P9-BZY-259

An American's Guide to Doing Business in
China

- **Negotiating contracts and agreements**
- **Understanding culture and customs**
- **Marketing products and services**

Mike Saxon, M.B.A.

A
BUSINESS
Avon, Massachusetts

Published by
Adams Media, an F+W Publications Company
57 Littlefield Street, Avon, MA 02322. U.S.A.
www.adamsmedia.com

ISBN 10: 1-59337-730-4
ISBN 13: 978-1-59337-730-4

Printed in the United States of America.

J I H G F E D C B A

Library of Congress Cataloging-in-Publication Data
Saxon, Mike.
An American's guide to doing business in China / Mike Saxon.
p.   cm.
ISBN-13: 978-1-59337-730-4
ISBN-10: 1-59337-730-4
1. International business enterprises—China. 2. Investments, Foreign—China. 3. China—Commerce. I. Title.
HD2910.S39 2007
330.951—dc22
2006028140

This publication is designed to provide accurate and authoritative information with regard to the subject matter covered. It is sold with the understanding that the publisher is not engaged in rendering legal, accounting, or other professional advice. If legal advice or other expert assistance is required, the services of a competent professional person should be sought.
—From a *Declaration of Principles* jointly adopted by a Committee of the American Bar Association and a Committee of Publishers and Associations

Many of the designations used by manufacturers and sellers to distinguish their product are claimed as trademarks. Where those designations appear in this book and Adams Media was aware of a trademark claim, the designations have been printed with initial capital letters.

Map of China on page 236 provided by Mike Saxon.

This book is available at quantity discounts for bulk purchases.
For information, please call 1-800-289-0963.

CONTENTS

227 Appendixes

INTRODUCTION

MUCH HAS BEEN WRITTEN about China lately, hyping the business opportunities now available in that country. The truth is that there really are many great opportunities there. In order to take advantage of them, though, you will first need to run a gauntlet of obstacles, ones for which you may be unprepared. My goal in this book is to prepare you for the challenges that await you and to offer specific advice that will allow you to seize those opportunities, while avoiding the pitfalls. Most of the material here comes from my own direct experience, and that of my company, China Business Partners (*www.chinabusinesspartners.com*).

One source of information on China that I would like to specifically recognize for its excellent research and statistics-gathering is the *Wall Street Journal*. The *WSJ* has printed many a story about different aspects of life in China that have informed the discussion here, and I recommend it as one of the best sources for keeping up to date on changes in China.

In recent years, Americans have been overly enthusiastic about China. Encouraged by a government eager for foreign capital and technology, and entranced by the prospect of 1.3 billion consumers, thousands of American and other foreign firms have rushed into the Chinese market without fully investigating the market situation, performing the necessary risk assessment, or getting expert advice. Without the necessary preparation, these companies and individuals often enter into bad business deals. The result is lost time, lost opportunity, and lost money.

The odds that any new business venture will succeed in China are far worse than the odds you would face in the

United States. You will be in a strange environment, with inadequate communication skills, few places to find help, and without key contacts or friends.

You may have heard many stories of business people succeeding in China. Many Americans have succeeded there, to be sure, but many more have failed and very few have succeeded on their first try.

Whatever you want to do in China—buy or sell something, have something made, find a partner, open a business, invest money, or anything else—the basic rule to know is this: Reaching an acceptable agreement to do anything is not the end. Murphy's laws, in all their forms, definitely apply here. It will take far longer to achieve your goal than you think, and it will take far more effort, time, money, and attention than you are planning. Don't assume that anything will happen unless you pull it through.

You must check on progress constantly and personally until you reach your goals. Then you must put fail-safe systems in place that assure continued performance up to the standards you have set.

While reform is absolutely essential for China to fully participate in the world trading community, in many areas these changes have not yet taken place. Companies must deal with the current environment in a realistic manner. Risk must be clearly evaluated. If a company determines that the risk is too great, it should seek other opportunities.

China has undergone an incredible transformation from a hostile, secretive, and insular country to a seemingly friendly and open one that welcomes you (and your money), and will, in many cases, grant you favors.

China's outward attitude change has resulted in accession to the World Trade Organization (WTO), a change that brings many new opportunities. Some have described it as "the beginning of time" for trade relations, because of the plethora of changes that China has already made and has agreed to make in the future in its laws, rules, regulations, and attitudes regarding foreign investment and trade. Problems will not disappear overnight, but instead of the traditional protectionism, free trade is the order of the day.

How to Use This Book

Within *An American's Guide to Doing Business in China*, how-to advice is given freely if it might show you a path to success that you may not be aware of. Sometimes you will learn of possible scenarios without being offered a specific course of action. When specific actions to take are suggested, realize that those recommendations are based on years of experience with American and Chinese firms doing business, from both sides of the fence and in the middle. I've seen what works and what doesn't, and I've set out to arm you for the travails ahead.

The book is organized so that you may read some sections without having to read other application sections that may not interest you. Some general sections (basically, Part One and Part Two and much of Part Three) should be pertinent to many applications, and everyone who is interested in doing business in China should read them. Other sections of Part Three, as well as Part Four, may be of interest depending on the type of business you are involved in.

Part One starts with points of common interest about China, including China's evolving role in the world, general issues an American faces in being there, and some background, perspectives, and trends on political, economic, and legal issues (including some forecasting as to where current trends will lead).

Next up, Part Two discusses other topics of importance to anyone doing business in China, such as the problems of dealing with the language barrier (Chapter 3), important and unique cultural issues (Chapter 4), and a detailed coverage of Chinese customs and how they will impact you (Chapter 5). The last three chapters of Part Two cover financial, legal, and import/export issues, along with the very important subject of what you need to know before embarking on a trip to China.

The chapters in Part Three aim to provide you with the skills and inside knowledge you need to succeed in such areas as sourcing, establishing an operating company, marketing, investing, negotiating, and managing your enterprise in China. Each category of business activity is discussed separately; namely, looking for established manufacturers from whom to purchase some kind of product, whether of your design or theirs (Chapter 9); setting up your own operations in China to manufacture or warehouse, as a wholly owned firm or with partners (Chapter 10); selling product in China, whether directly or through channels (Chapter 11); and making investments in China, whether in existing companies, trading on an exchange (in China these companies are called "published"), or through private financial transactions (Chapter 12). The last chapter of Part Three covers what you need to know to negotiate successfully in China and to maintain relationships after the negotiations.

In Part Four, you'll learn about the many different areas of business opportunities available in China, including, in Chapter 15, some of the fastest-growing and most promising ones. The various Appendixes will provide you with all sorts of information useful for anyone doing business in or traveling to China. After reading this book, you should be well aware of the opportunities and hazards to be found by Americans doing business in China, and perhaps you will be on the road to creating a successful venture of your own.

Part One

An Introduction to China

You have taken a major step forward by buying this book. You're saying a lot about yourself. You are serious about doing business in China. You recognize the realities of the global economy, and that making money in the future may depend on your ability to utilize resources outside this country.

In spite of the statistic that 22 percent of all of China's imports are from America, higher than the number of imports from any other country, America does not dominate the Chinese business world. You'll find a very strong representation of products, advertising, presence, and influence from Japan as well as from Germany, Sweden, and other countries.

Americans have long been too insular. While large American multinational firms have learned the benefits of worldwide business, most small businesses have not. Many believe that doing business in China is beyond their ability and resources. They are now discovering that, in many cases, only by dealing internationally can they survive.

In Part One, you'll learn about the basic issues and problems that you will face when doing business in China. International business, especially in China, presents a whole range of challenges different from those found in the United States. However, it is not beyond your reach. If you exert the effort, and study the culture, customs, and languages, you will not only survive, you will prosper.

Chapter 1

Basic Facts and Background

ALTHOUGH THERE IS RESISTANCE, most Americans now realize that we are in a global economy. Whether we like it or not, America can't be isolated any longer without giving up much of what we cherish. For a multitude of reasons, such as developments in communications, and economic interactions and interdependencies, we are now part of a global economy that cannot be reversed. Countries as well as companies realize that specialization and partnering are the order of the day.

Not very many years ago, a company performed every business function internally. If you had an idea to make a product, you set up some kind of manufacturing facility, maybe in your garage or kitchen. You had to plan your business; design your product or service; raise capital; buy your raw materials, machinery, equipment, and supplies; hire people; sell the product; stock inventory; carry accounts receivable; and keep records of all these transactions.

Now, companies have learned to concentrate on their core business and outsource other operations and services to people who are specialists in providing specific functions. Countries are becoming specialists also. America is a consuming nation, with most people now employed in services.

When American companies started outsourcing to other countries, Mexico was their favorite destination. Wage rates were much lower, tariffs and other trade impediments were being lifted, Mexico was close, many companies already had a partly Hispanic work force, and many Americans already had some familiarity with the Spanish language or could quickly find bilingual people to ease communications difficulties.

However, the trend toward outsourcing accelerated so swiftly, and our economy is so vast, that it quickly absorbed Mexico's excess labor. The two countries that are now most thought about when discussing outsourcing are countries with labor pools so large that they won't be fully utilized for a long time—China and India.

India's prime advantage over China is language. Most Indians speak English. It is more ingrained into their society. Language difficulties are a great barrier to working in China. India is becoming the destination of choice for language-oriented jobs, such as customer service and other customer-contact work and other activities requiring communication.

On the other hand, China has many advantages in manufacturing. The transportation and public-utilities infrastructure needed for manufacturing is being built more rapidly in China. Also, the literacy rate in China is higher and the government is friendlier to foreigners in general and Americans in particular.

China is the best manufacturing outsource destination in the world today. In fact, China has already become the leading producing nation in the world.

Production costs in China for most products are much lower than they are elsewhere. China has a vast labor pool that costs a fraction of what America's does (about one-ninth, but this varies from area to area; see Appendix 12 for wage rates by province and region).

Since labor remains a significant part of manufacturing costs, and American hourly labor costs are eight to ten times higher than those in China, automation cannot make up all of the difference. Unless there are extenuating circumstances, American manufacturing is less likely to be economical.

Furthermore, because of the differences in direct labor costs, and other factors, most other costs are also lower in China. Because labor is a major part of construction costs, and building codes are much less stringent, building costs are much lower than they are in the United States, and because taxes and land costs are also much lower, so are occupancy costs. Utility, insurance, and most business service costs are also less, as are most other costs.

Another factor making China's manufacturing costs lower is the sharply reduced regulatory cost involved in meeting government codes for environmental and safety concerns. Some of the related costs that are higher outside of China are effective waste disposal; installation of all manner of safety devices and precautions; building standards; health costs; handicap considerations; environmental maintenance and aesthetic issues that incur related costs (billboard regulation, for example); regeneration requirements; and so on.

On the down side, China's lower standards bring with them societal or hidden costs, ones that are being incurred now and will have to be paid later either in real terms or in degradation of the quality of life. To be sure, China is beginning to recognize the importance of some of these issues, and new laws and regulations will have an increasing impact in the future. For example, Beijing is now starting to enforce new environmental rules.

Taxes in China also are far less than they are in the United States. You will find nowhere near the number of hidden taxes that face you in America. There is no sales tax, utility tax, gas tax, and so on. Corporate income taxes are much less. In some cases, with the application of tax credits for exporting, income taxes almost disappear.

China does have some costs that we do not have in the United States. One major one is the cost of getting favorable and expedited government attention.

A Growing Infrastructure

China is just now building the infrastructure necessary to support the industrial giant that it has already become. According to government figures, China's infrastructure investment is currently growing at a 22.8 percent annual rate.

If you haven't been to China, or if it's been years since your last visit, or you did not have the time to observe and compare the "goings-on" then and now, you will be utterly amazed at what's happening and the changes being wrought in that country.

To truly chronicle all the changes that have occurred would have required making scores of trips over the past decade, employing "time-lapse" photography, and taking copious notes with hundreds of detailed observations.

In almost every phase of development, the differences are truly astounding. For example, six years ago, a trip in Guangdong Province from Shenzhen to Guangzhou by car took almost six hours. On the way, there was not one piece of farm equipment to be seen, or a commercial vehicle of any kind in the fields. There were several cars, and a large number of donkeys and oxen, but mostly people were doing their work with manual tools.

Two years ago, on that same itinerary, the highways had been greatly expanded, overpasses had been added, and many other improvements had been made. Despite a great increase in highway traffic, the trip took only two and a half hours. Several pieces of farm equipment and a great number of farm trucks could be seen along the way.

This year, on the same trip, there were too many farm equipment vehicles to count. There were also countless pieces of construction equipment, with many major projects in progress. Large tracts of land were being leveled. The trip by car now takes two hours, even with much-increased traffic. Highways have been improved more than enough to handle the additional vehicles.

Cities and economic zones throughout China are undergoing the same type of transformation. There is literally about one construction project on every major city block. China has stated its official growth rate at about 9 percent per year. In economic zones, the growth rate is far greater, although in the more populated inland areas, growth rates have spurted upward in the last few years.

There are great disadvantages to a dictatorship, of course. But China may be in a unique position to be able to demonstrate the advantages of a progressive, logical dictatorship. In an authoritarian environment, you do have the power to make and implement decisions quickly and efficiently. Many American businessmen find it easier to deal with the Chinese government than with democratic ones, which have many more considerations and variables. China is focused on trade and business development, and the government can often cut through many problems to achieve an end result.

Despite the obvious drawbacks to being an "emerging" country, there are distinct advantages as well. If you are a keen observer of history, you can predict what has worked and what has not worked in other, more economically advanced countries. To give one example: Because China did not have the enormous investment in established wired-technology telephone systems, the country was able to leapfrog normal developmental steps and go directly to cellular technology. Today China is the leading nation in the use of cellular phones.

The same goes for transportation infrastructure: China was able to emphasize air transportation over ground transportation. Airports are cheaper to build than are highways, and building them takes China into the twenty-first century faster. That is not to say that China is not greatly improving its roads and other land infrastructure; the highways being built also take advantage of twenty-first-century technology.

Labor and Other Costs: China's Secret

Some people think that doing business in China is a panacea for all their problems. If they have a product made in China it will satisfy their needs at a lower cost. China is not a panacea, but the country does have one great advantage over the rest of the world: it has an extremely large supply of educated, *cheap* labor. That is its magic. China's labor force is not better organized, smarter, more creative, or more capable than anyone else's; as a matter of fact, the workers are not nearly as experienced, as well trained in advanced techniques, or as adaptable as the American labor force. But because labor is still such an overpowering factor in costs today, its one advantage still more than overcomes its shortcomings.

One point that will take on greater significance as time goes on is that the huge advantage in labor cost that businesses in China have is hindering them from doing more to fix their shortcomings. Businesses can avoid fixing other problems and still operate economically. The labor-rate advantage masks other deficiencies.

History tells us that over time things will change. Labor rates will move closer together, and manufacturing costs will become much more competitive. In China's case, the labor resources are so vast that it will take a long time to reach that point; however, it is estimated that more than 150 million people from China's rural areas have joined the work force in urban areas in the last five years, and that rate shows no signs of decreasing yet.

There is another side of this coin to consider. People who work with China for the first time will find that they are, to some extent, trading one problem for others.

While the direct price may be cheaper, there are many hidden costs that will be incurred to attain that lower cost. These hidden costs include mistakes due to miscommunication, misunderstandings, and different customs, ethics (tendency to cut corners when not directly supervised), and standards. China has some costs that we do not have here, including, as mentioned, the cost of getting favorable and expedited government attention—or failing that, the cost of *not* getting favorable and expedited attention.

Then there are hidden costs involved in attaining contracts and motivating employees and others helping in your venture, as well as the costs in time, attention, and money that it takes to conclude successful agreements and to set up, supervise, and monitor their performance.

You will see in the following pages that failure to invest in these extra activities greatly increases your risk of performance failure, regardless of any agreements. (See Chapter 13 for guidance on negotiation and other pertinent topics.)

Recognize the hidden costs and constantly factor them into your equation at the same time that you are working to minimize them.

Health Issues

Many—perhaps most—Americans who visit China experience some kind of malady. Almost every visitor to China reports that the incidence of sickness is far greater in China than at home. Furthermore, the limited statistics available show that the Chinese people themselves seem much more prone to colds, flus, and food-related illnesses than are their counterparts in America. The question is, what has triggered these health problems, and how do we prevent them? This became particularly critical during the SARS crisis. Interviews with a number of Americans who have experienced health problems, as well as with doctors both in the United States and in China, provide some possible answers.

Avoiding Viruses

The doctors interviewed agree that when you are in China your immune system is not nearly as effective as that of a Chinese person, who has had constant exposure to the bacteria base in that country. The most common sources from which you may pick up a virus are personal contact, air, water, and food.

For protection against problems arising from personal contact, carry packages of cleansing wipes imbued with disinfectant (available at any drugstore), and use them discreetly following contacts. Also, pay special attention to washing or disinfecting your hands at every opportunity, with special care after using bathroom facilities. It's a good idea to carry toilet paper and seat covers with you.

Other than wearing a mask, there is little you can do about airborne bacteria. Airplanes have been mentioned as a possible source of health problems, especially if they recirculate air. On the ground or in the air, if someone is coughing or sneezing near you, it is wise to move away or at least turn away.

Don't drink tap water. Bottled water is readily available almost everywhere in China now, so you should not drink the water served at a restaurant unless it is bottled.

However, food is the most probable culprit for transmitting health problems; this conclusion is based on personal experiences and test cases. Don't experiment with small or little-known restaurants unless your hosts highly recommend them. Four- or five-star hotels usually have good and safe fare.

The Chinese have a custom of business or formal dining that includes ordering a variety of different dishes and placing them on a large lazy-Susan-type tray. The tray revolves around the table, so that everyone can partake of every dish. The problem is that most dishes do not have a serving utensil devoted to that dish, so that people serve themselves from the various dishes with the same chopsticks that they eat with. This practically ensures that you will be sharing bacteria with others at the table.

Fortunately, the Chinese also have the custom of allowing their guests to taste each new dish first. To be safe, you should take from untouched dishes what you think you will want before others have the opportunity to dip into it, and don't take second helpings. Then order a special side dish as an adjunct, if needed.

Many people pick up some kind of health problem about once every three times they visit, but after following the practice of not eating from common dishes without serving utensils, the incidence of health problems is generally greatly reduced.

If You Do Get Sick

If you do catch something in spite of all precautions, you can take comfort in knowing that China does have a great health-care system. Be sure, though, to take someone with you who can interpret for you.

Despite what you may have heard, the facilities of the better hospitals are very clean, their staff is very competent, their prices are very low by our standards (perhaps one-tenth of what they are in the United States), and they give Americans special attention. Just as in the United States, the quality of staff does vary from hospital to hospital, so ask your host or someone you know there which are the best hospitals in your city.

One negative is that for most of the common ailments (flu and colds), the common medicines used in China are not nearly as effective as the medicines used in the United States, and the medicines are usually administered intravenously. I take a bottle of strong anti-viral pills with me just in case, but if you have an injury or would just like a doctor's opinion for any problem, don't hesitate to go to a good hospital.

Safety

Many Americans are reluctant to do business with China because they fear operating under the authority of a Communist government. In fact, if you are simply buying legal goods from China, or having legal products made there on your specifications, you will probably not have much contact with the government. It will be much as it is in the United States, where you normally don't think about the government.

If you want to make investments, or are running or set-ting up a business or marketing products in China, there is much that you need to know about the government. These subjects are discussed in other chapters, but this is really not a safety issue.

For the most part, the government is very friendly. It realizes that China needs foreign capital and goodwill to build its economy. The government's attitude toward for-eigners is very favorable. You will also find the police very friendly and accommodating. On more than one occasion Americans have said they have received favored treatment, such as being allowed to enter a barricaded entrance or a street, solely because they are American.

Once in a while, especially on government-sponsored tours, you may get an overzealous guide who harangues Americans about our country's support for Taiwan indepen-dence and other political issues, but for the most part, you are safe from political harassment.

Many people are afraid of China because it is a Commu-nist country and because its justice system seems too harsh and arbitrary, and they may feel they could be in physical danger from the government. In fact, I do not know of a single businessperson on legitimate business who has been harassed by the government.

One common question prospective visitors have is about crime in China. Yes, there is crime, and because of the lack of accurate reporting, exactly how much is not known.

According to government statistics, juvenile (under age 18) crime has been up an average of 14 percent per year from 2000 to 2004, and up 23 percent in 2005; but remember that it is up from an almost zero base. There is also some reported gang activity. The younger generation apparently does not fear the government as much as its parents did.

However, there are very few violent crimes. Violent crimes are dealt with in the harshest manner, and crimes against foreigners carry even greater penalties. You can still feel much safer in China than you can in most large cities in the United States. During years of travel to China, I have not encountered or heard of violent crimes against Americans. On the other hand, if you are planning to do something illegal, like buying or possessing drugs, you can expect incredibly harsh sentences.

Private statements against government actions or policies are easily tolerated, but don't get up on a soapbox in Tiananmen Square and rail against the government. To avoid embarrassment or animosity, the best course to take is to be apolitical while you are in China. You should not worry, though, that you will be in serious danger simply for expressing your opinion.

Information and Statistics

China is not and never has been an information society. The Chinese press is not free, and the government will not tolerate serious or potentially serious opposition to its decisions, policies, authority, or form of government.

Because of government control of the press, and its policy of publishing only what it wants the public to know, you cannot rely heavily on published statistics or the accuracy of news. First of all, China does not keep statistics regularly and accurately. Accuracy and thoroughness are not as important as the need to save face. Historically, unfavorable statistics such as traffic fatalities, number of deaths from disasters, and crime statistics have been sizably underreported.

However, in a recent move that, hopefully, has broad implications, the National Administration for the Protection of State Secrets and the Ministry of Civil Affairs decided that releasing information about disasters would no longer be illegal. The public's right to know is becoming stronger, as long as it doesn't threaten the current political order.

The lack of accurate, formalized statistics becomes most important to you when you are researching anything or trying to find sources. In America you can get specific information sources, and you know what they contain, how to use them, and where to find them. There are information sources everywhere—libraries, research facilities, and so on. A plethora of companies large and small sell information of all kinds in all forms and formats. For most information in the United States, there are duplicate sources. America has become an information society. From early school years, Americans are trained to conduct research. Our institutions, companies, and even individuals keep statistics. There are many areas of official statistics with guidelines and even laws governing how statistics are gathered and recorded. You can usually trust most sources to be reasonably accurate and complete. America is a statistical society.

China is neither a statistical nor an information society. It has no library system, no public research facilities, and no penchant for statistical accuracy and completeness. Children are not trained to conduct research or to seek sources of information. Because China has only recently been somewhat intellectually free, you will not find the seeking of information, or the expectation of access to information that Americans have. In China, sources of information have not had time to develop and mature, although there are nascent signs that this will improve.

Chapter 2

Perspective on China

TWO VERY SIGNIFICANT EVENTS for China occurred in 2001. One was the awarding of the 2008 Olympic Games to China, which happened in July 2001. Another was China's entry into the WTO in December of the same year. These two events deeply affected China's destiny and its self-image.

China is the oldest culture on earth, once known for its creativity and admired by other nations. In the modern world, China has been seen as a second-class nation. Being awarded the Olympic Games and entering the WTO marked China's acceptance by the world as a powerful, prestigious nation. The pride of everyone in China, from the commoner to the highest official, in hosting the 2008 Olympics cannot be overestimated. (To see the official Olympics Web site, go to *www.beijing-2008.org*.) The 2008 Olympics in China will be a huge success. China cannot accept anything less. The whole country has been preparing for it and has been anticipating it since it was first announced. The staging of the Games is meant to say to the world that China has arrived, and that it is a nation to be reckoned with once again.

China's own athletes will probably excel at the 2008 Olympics. The country has a very thorough and modern training program to prepare its athletes for international competition. The Chinese athletes will likely be first in both total medals and gold medals, and they will win events they have never won before. China's national pride is at stake.

This emphasis on the Olympics is making people all over China more aware of sports in general. That awareness can be used to advance some sports-related business concepts.

The other major event of 2001—China's entry into the WTO—has served to announce the importance of China as a trading partner, its embrace of the concept of free trade, and its acceptance by the world. It has also given China's fledgling business community confidence in the country's future economic policies and direction.

The Political Climate

There is a widely held belief in the West that political and economic freedom must go together. China is trying to disprove that belief.

In China, public opinion is not sought after or followed, as it is in the United States. In discussing the attitudes of the Chinese, we must distinguish between the government and the people.

The government is very difficult to predict. There are certain actions and behaviors that usually succeed in achieving an objective with the government, but government policy can change in an instant. If that happens, whatever has been agreed upon no longer stands. The government seldom takes back its actions, but it often takes back words and perceived promises. Government people in China think and act differently than the general population, making them less predictable.

Unlike in America, where people support government policies whether they voted for them or not, the Chinese people do not see themselves as having any responsibility for the government. They are acted upon by the government. They are resigned to being ruled by the government.

The attitudes and many of the observations and comments made in this book are about the *people*, not the government. Many of the older people (over age 55) have strong memories of repression, but most people, while inwardly decrying the stupidity of individual rules or laws or the direction that the government is taking, are absolutely resigned to accepting governmental rule.

Don't count on revolution in China, but rather evolution. Of course, that means stability and safety, at least from the risks associated with some other less stable governments.

What Americans perceive as rights, the Chinese see as privileges, which makes them more accepting and tolerant of problems. They point to the string of economic successes and the memories of much harder times as proof that the government is on the right road.

Because of the successes of liberalized economic policies, further encouragement of free, private enterprise can be expected. On the other hand, don't expect liberalized political policies.

To the Chinese people, freedom means something different than what it means to us. Clearly, the people are much freer in most areas than they have been in the past, but they do not have freedom of political thought. They can speak out against rules and regulations and can criticize the effects the rules have had, but they are not free to try to change the system of government that made those rules, or to engage in any organized action, such as a demonstration or assembly. In China, there is no right of assembly.

While economic and political freedom may go hand in hand in America, the government in China has no intention of democratizing the country or even of gradually allowing too much more popular influence in the government. The thing China's leaders most fear is popular participation that would challenge the governmental decision-making process.

However, Beijing has learned some valuable lessons. The Chinese leaders have shown themselves to be intelligent, heuristic managers, but they remain steadfast in their beliefs. They have learned that putting forth a friendlier face to the world and to their own people is in their best interest. They have learned that granting freedom wherever it does not threaten their form of government is a very good idea. It frees administrators from some difficult decisions and some harsh criticism; it gives their people and foreigners the appearance of freedom; and most of all, it creates a more successful society.

Any appearance of freedom is in the government's best interest. Beijing is making some concessions to the public demand for participation. Regarding the question of how to narrow the income gap (discussed later in this chapter), the government chose 20 people from among 5,000 applicants to be heard on the subject. As unimpressive as this might seem to people in a democracy, to allow any public input is a major concession for China, which has shown few gestures in that direction.

The Chinese people seem to easily accept an autocratic government. There is no fomenting revolution, peaceful or otherwise, in the offing. Most people alive in China today are too young to remember the exceedingly oppressive policies of Mao Zedong's anti-intellectual movement and the millions of deaths caused by his autocratic leadership.

Censorship

People who think that freedom has come to China, or that freedom is on the way, should examine Chinese policy on censorship. The Chinese government, unlike that of the United States, takes a proactive role. China perceives the Internet as a political threat, because users could get news from independent sources and have virtual meetings and potentially mind-influencing political discussions outside government control. Consequently, the government has imposed certain censorship rules on the search engines, on pain of being banned from China altogether.

The government still controls the media and all content. Beijing decides what will be said, and when, and how. The government uses the media to put across its own opinions and policies.

The propaganda department of the Communist Party issues guidelines for different stories to the only official news agency, *Xinhua*, and if newspapers, television stations, news Web sites, and other sources of news in China want to avoid problems, they will follow those guidelines.

When China allowed Internet use to spread to the general population, many people thought it would bring an end to censorship. They thought that because of the inherent freedom of the Internet, it would be almost impossible to have effective censorship of it, even if Beijing wanted it. However, they miscalculated the priority the Chinese government places on control of any possible organized opposition to Communist rule. The Internet offered a forum that, if not strictly controlled, could be used to establish and promote free public thinking on politically sensitive issues, and eventually to organize and direct opposition to the government itself.

China has devoted whatever resources were necessary to control this potential threat. About 30,000 government-employed censors are now patrolling Internet use. There is a vast pool of Internet users in China, and the potential for many more users.

Beijing saw that it needed to control the search engines, many of which were foreign. It issued a veiled ultimatum to foreign search companies to acquiesce to restrictions or forgo the vast and developing Chinese market. The search companies chose to acquiesce. Therefore, there is the interesting scenario of American companies—the bastions of Internet freedom such as Microsoft, Yahoo, and Google—placed in the role of censors working for the Chinese government against computer users who are trying to learn more about topics such as democracy and political freedom, which the government forbids.

Microsoft's China-based Internet portal does not allow the words "democracy," "freedom," "human rights," "Taiwan," "Tibet," or "demonstration," or many other words that the government finds offensive for being politically sensitive, illegal, or pornographic. And in March 2005, new regulations were put in place that requires all China-based Web sites to be registered with the government.

In exchange for being allowed to do business in China, the American Internet giants have also cooperated with Beijing in its censorship efforts. Not surprisingly, most Americans do not know of this cooperation between freedom-espousing American Internet companies and the Chinese government in helping to quell any interest in the democratic process that Americans are supposedly trying to proliferate, since these companies downplay such disagreeable news from the American people on their news Web sites.

In September 2005, China imposed new regulations to control content on its news Web sites. These regulations were issued by the Ministry of Information Industry and China's cabinet, the State Council, to standardize the management of news and information. Sites can only post news about current events and politics, and at that, only "healthy and civilized news and information that is beneficial to [China's] economic development and conducive to social progress will be allowed." It is further stated that "Sites are prohibited from spreading news and information that goes against state security and public interest." Those laws, in the manner of other Chinese laws, are worded in such a way as to be open to interpretation.

A Chinese journalist received a ten-year sentence in September 2005 for criticizing media restrictions in an e-mail. Information used to convict him was furnished by Yahoo.

Another disturbing development for Americans is that Yahoo has taken to censoring the news it disseminates to us. The Reuters news story on the September 2005 incident was reproduced on Yahoo that morning, but it was quickly removed when Yahoo realized the story was critical of the company's cooperation with the Chinese government in the conviction of the Chinese journalist.

For those who might think this was an isolated incident, Yahoo repeated the scenario on the night of August 9, 2006. Yahoo initially reproduced another Reuters story, one regarding criticism from the group Human Rights Watch directed at Microsoft, Google, and Yahoo for their continued cooperation with the Chinese government in blocking politically sensitive Web sites and search terms. Yahoo removed the story within the hour, so that no mention of it was available the next morning.

China has closed thousands of cybercafés and installed cameras in them, and it requires registration with official identity cards for use. The government has now installed cameras in all cybercafés and has closed thousands of cybercafés that did not cooperate fully with their desire to punish what they call "misuse" of the Internet. Users who disregard governmental guidelines have found themselves quickly confronted at their cyberlocations by agents dispatched to investigate infractions.

Espionage

Some policymakers see China's growing economic power as a threat to the United States and to world peace. The FBI has put increasing emphasis on containing the Chinese espionage threat, which aims to gain both a military and an economic advantage.

One of the problems with this policy is that many times the businesses that may be targets see FBI involvement as an economic threat to doing business in China and an impediment to tapping technical expertise from the Chinese-American community.

Another problem is the methods that China uses in gathering information. It is not sending trained, paid agents to gather information in an organized fashion. It simply questions the hundreds of thousands of Chinese who visit and study in the United States and also tries to enlist the help of Chinese-Americans to provide certain information in an effort to help build the Chinese economy, appealing to nationalistic pride. The FBI estimates that there are about 150,000 Chinese students now studying in the United States, and about 700,000 Chinese visitors each year.

At this writing, more than ten individual industrial espionage cases perpetrated by China are currently active, and the FBI has obtained several convictions already. Convictions have proven difficult, though, because of the unconventional methods used, and the lack of cooperation of American companies in stemming the flow of information.

With moderate effort, the FBI could put together a solid case that there is a coordinated Chinese effort to obtain technological secrets. The FBI has identified 3,000 Chinese front companies set up in the United States specifically to gather technologies illegally.

The FBI might be well advised to prepare a short well-documented professional presentation to educate companies that might unwittingly allow the Chinese to acquire proprietary information. Such a presentation could show the seemingly harmless methods Beijing uses to obtain confidential information and the detrimental consequences to those they acquire it from. This would go a long way toward securing the cooperation of American companies.

U.S.-China Relations

The impact of China's growing economic power on the United States is hard to predict. There are many unknown variables. Of course, China's actions speak much louder than its words, which in many cases mean nothing. China's apparent goal is to become the foremost world power. The government believes that it is destined to achieve that goal. Michael Pillsbury, a high-level adviser to our State Department and the Pentagon, says, "China sees the U.S. as a military rival." He further asserts that "Beijing sees the U.S. as an inevitable foe, and is planning accordingly."

China realizes that it needs economic power to achieve its goals of domination. Many people argue that increasing trade and economic interdependence means more understanding and more cooperation on other issues. History shows us that while there is some merit to this point of view, economic interdependence by itself will not eliminate conflicts.

Many Americans believe that, sooner or later, the ideas and culture flowing from the West will get through to the Chinese people, and they will change their politics. However, experience has demonstrated that an autocratic government can maintain power for an indefinite period, as long as it is dedicated enough and ruthless enough to continue to exercise complete control of the political thoughts of its population. Furthermore, if the people are becoming continually more prosperous, they have much less desire to change their government.

In many ways, China is a much more dangerous opponent than others the United States has faced in the past. Beijing has learned something that most autocratic governments never learn. Most totalitarian governments suppress all forms of free thought. That usually produces poverty, which in turn means that the government isn't likely to have the economic means to achieve its foreign policy goals for long.

What does this mean in terms of possible future conflicts? China has a burning ambition to be dominant. The Chinese "attitude" comes from the government and is planned and deliberate. The leaders know where they want to go and they will do whatever it takes to get there, without much concern for moral or ethical restrictions.

Most Chinese businesspeople connect economic freedoms to political freedoms, and are convinced that the next regime after the current leader, Hu Jintao, will move toward political freedoms. Unfortunately, there is no hard evidence for that scenario at all.

In less publicized actions, the Chinese leaders demonstrate that if their form of government is threatened in any way, "human rights" is not a consideration and punishment is swift and harsh. Consider their constant censorship of all potentially threatening forms of political expression and their perennial tightening of laws in the political area. While their enforcement of political laws is strict, it is in contrast to the lax and uneven enforcement of many other laws and regulations in the commercial sector.

The government understands that keeping the people happy and prosperous is necessary to achieve its long-term goals. It is increasingly perceptive about separating the freedoms and actions that are politically threatening from those that are not. The government is allowing more popular input into decisions that are not politically sensitive, fostering the view that it is loosening its grip, when, in fact, it has not done so yet.

Americans need to recognize the underlying facts, but that does not mean we need to be an enemy to China's growth. We can facilitate China's economic growth, while at the same time remaining mindful of the need to maintain our technological superiority by safeguarding our chief assets—the intellectual, intangible assets, such as education, research, and technology.

It is also possible to seek to encourage those few signs of change that appear more democratic, such as the increased participation of non-government people in the decision-making process and the loosening of restrictions on the dissemination of information.

It should be noted, though, that as China's economic power grows, it will be emboldened to make political demands. Beijing will use its economic power to build military might. It will spend increasing amounts on China's military, and until the government changes its political goals or until it is persuaded that it can achieve the image and status it seeks without military might, China will remain a threat to the United States.

Official figures of Chinese military expenditures have been expanding at an annual rate of about 10 percent since the 1980s, when China's economic growth started in earnest. Some military experts estimate that actual defense expenditures are probably closer to expanding at 20–30 percent annually. If these expenditures are truly defensive, what military threat does China perceive?

Neither the mass of Chinese people, nor the Chinese culture, is bellicose. Either a change in government attitude or a democratic China would remove the China threat.

The Capitalist-Communist Compromise

One should not confuse economic liberalization with political liberalization or democracy. China is still a Communist dictatorship, despite its tremendous successes in Hong Kong and the benefits Hong Kong has brought to China after the turnover of that city to Mainland China's rule. China is again quashing Hong Kong's push to democratize further and has made it clear in many political statements that economic liberalization does not change the political system.

China's government has tended to be mercantilist and protectionist. China has made significant progress toward a market-oriented economy, but parts of its bureaucracy still tend to protect domestic business and state-owned firms from imports, while encouraging exports. WTO accession and economic success are helping in this area.

China has the remnants of a planned economy. In many sectors of the Chinese business community, the understanding of free enterprise and competition is incomplete. The Chinese economy is often prone to overinvestment and overproduction, for reasons not related to supply and demand.

On a trip to China several years ago, a U.S. delegation was asked a question by Chinese businessmen: "How much of business in America is owned by the government?" It took several minutes of conversation for the Americans to understand the question. When the Chinese were told "None," they couldn't comprehend the answer. Private enterprise is a relatively new concept in China and the government still owns a large share of the largest enterprises. This is rapidly changing, however.

It is only in the last twenty-some years that the Chinese government has taken a practical approach to the economy and has devoted itself to achieving success at building it by whatever means work, as opposed to the hard-line, dogmatic Communist philosophy of central rule.

This has led to a capitalistic shift in direction and a clear dichotomy in philosophy—a capitalist economic direction with a Communist political direction. As long as the leadership puts a high priority on economic growth, the recent successes that China has had in economic growth, job growth, income growth, and increased wealth will continue.

Economic Growth

In the 1950s, Mao Zedong declared that the Chinese economy would surpass that of Britain by 1970, and the U.S. economy by the 1980s. In fact, Mao's draconian policies dragged the country down and suppressed progress for many years, while the Western countries' economies prospered, widening the economic chasm between China and the West dramatically.

Because China remains a Communist country, all laws, policies, rule, and regulations are set by the central government. However, since Mao Zedong's death in 1976, government economic policy has been much more pragmatic. Since about 1979, the government has embarked on a course to steer the country more and more toward free enterprise.

Those policies have been successful beyond anyone's wildest expectations, and China has joined fully in the increased economic prosperity of the world. China has enjoyed an economic growth rate that has exceeded every other country's and has been remarkable for its longevity.

Early economic policy was influenced by China's own early successes, as well as, to some extent, the experiences of other cultural Chinese economies such as Hong Kong, Taiwan, and Singapore.

As the leadership has changed and become more experienced with these radically different economic policies and more flexible in implementing policies that worked, rather than following dogmatic principles, a new philosophy of pragmatism has developed. China has consulted with the foremost experts in the world in regard to which policies work and which policies don't. It has studied the economies of the United States and Europe and has crafted its recent policies from the economic policies and the results of policies of the economically successful countries.

China's leaders have eschewed the old Communist dogma that capitalists have nothing to teach them. The new doctrine is that economic success brings more power and actually helps to perpetuate the political system by satisfying the needs of the people for economic advancement.

Certainly accession to the WTO was one of the instigative events that pushed China to change many of its laws, rules, and regulations faster than it might have, but the leadership had already opted for change before the country's entry into the WTO.

China's "economic miracle" has been very cleverly constructed by a very intelligent group of people following successful examples of what others have done before them.

Once the central government made the philosophical transition, admitting that the Communist economic system could not match the capitalist system, progress was rapid. The Chinese have had a road map. They never had to reinvent a wheel—they just used wheels that other people had invented. They got competent experts in developed countries to advise them on how to avoid the mistakes of other countries and how to encourage the huge foreign investment that was required.

With the enlightened policies of modern China, the country's economy has grown more than 9 percent in 2005 and has had an annual inflation-adjusted growth rate of more than 8 percent for the last twenty-five years, while the U.S. economy has grown by a rate of 3 percent over the same time period.

There are several reasons why China's growth rate could be so high for so long. China had a lower base to start with and had much more room to grow. China had many unemployed and underemployed people, so that dynamic growth was not accompanied by substantial wage-rate increases and inflation. China's wage rates were much lower than those of any industrialized country, and because labor was and is one of the largest ingredients in manufacturing, lower wages and a business-friendly government attract investment and business.

The Biggest Economy?

If the growth rates continue, China's economy will overtake the U.S. economy at some point. No trend continues on the same path forever, though, and it has become a game to predict when, if ever, China will become the largest economy in the world.

Some economists say never, and others give estimates mostly between twenty and forty years, but most say that the China factor will be the most important element in changing the economics of the world. If China's population is more than four times that of the United States, then it follows that even if each Chinese worker earned a fraction of what each American earned, their total earnings could exceed ours. Predicting requires many assumptions, and behind each assumption is a risk.

Let's lay out some of these suppositions.

First, keeping growth rates about the same assumes that neither the United States nor China makes basic changes in its patterns of taxation, education, business and antitrust laws, regulations, and incentives. In other words, that the business and education environments remain fairly constant. It is reasonably certain they will not.

Second, China does not have nearly as many large businesses as the United States. Its growth has been much more dependent on small business, and small business tends to grow at a faster rate than big business. Also, in the United States, because of the power, influence, and money of big business, we have allowed a big-business bias to creep into the political and economic process. Laws and regulations in the United States now favor big business both overtly and subtly. If China's laws become more restrictive or if U.S. laws move to be friendlier to small business, growth rates may change.

Also, there is a difference in business "quality." There is a higher technology level, and a higher management and worker skill level in the United States. China is aware of this need to create domestic-based technology, and to increase both worker and management skills. How this will all play out will also affect economic growth.

Besides the built-in factors that will affect comparative growth rates, there are other unknowns. How will China perform when there is no longer a clear road map and the country will have to progress based on its own innovative policies? When China reaches that point, it will be on an untraveled road and its management problems will multiply.

While China has become adept at copying the successful policies of others, it has not yet shown that it is equally adept at innovating successful policies. Indeed, China's culture and experience, which have served it so well to this point, will gravitate against a world of innovations.

The Chinese will have to learn to be evenhanded in their dealings, to be empathetic, to freely admit mistakes, to become educated in areas where they have never had a need for knowledge, and to build an infrastructure not only of the tangibles of steel and concrete, but also of the intangibles of advanced education, information, and research. It is problematic as to whether they will be able or even willing to do this.

There is another overriding factor in predicting future economic growth. As unthinkable as it sounds, at some point in the not-too-distant future, China will run out of people to become the low-level workers upon which it can cheaply continue to build its economy. Already, the educated and experienced among the migrant workers are demanding higher wages than their predecessors.

A classic supply/demand labor market is in the offing. First, the management, engineering, and specialist groups will experience the beginning of shortages. Studying the labor-pool figures compared to expected manpower needs leads to the possibility that not twenty to forty years from now, but within perhaps seven to ten years, the basic labor pool will begin to experience competition and significantly higher wages.

What happens then will depend on the government's recognition of the situation and its reaction to it. Along with all the other factors, a squeezing of the labor supply would change China's growth rates significantly.

Back to the present, though. The enormous body of work that was needed in China in such areas as business law was Herculean, and, though much work remains, the progress has been remarkable. China's economic growth has been spectacular and the government can be extremely proud of its now-established record of accomplishment.

The Next Five-Year Plan

In October 2005, China's Central Committee, the CPC, formulated its next Five-Year Plan, covering 2006–2010. The CPC claims that the plan is more scientifically based than any plan in the past, and that scientific development will also be the guide in the whole process of China's reform and drive to open up.

Premier Wen Jiabao points to the early achievement of many of the goals of the last Five-Year Plan (2000–2005) and says that its stated long-term goal of doubling its 2000 per capita gross domestic product (GDP) figure by 2010 is on target.

The premier also called for more efforts to build a harmonious society, saying that employment, social security, poverty reduction, education, medical care, environmental protection, and safety will be given priority.

On social security, the premier called for further efforts to improve the pension system, basic medical care, unemployment, industrial injuries, and maternity care; to earnestly resolve the social security issue for migrant farm workers in cities; and to set up a security system of minimum living standards for rural areas.

The new Five-Year Plan focuses on agriculture and energy. It strives to improve energy efficiency (with a specific goal of reducing energy costs per unit by 20 percent), protect the environment, and continue to assiduously build infrastructure. It also specifically recognizes the income gap between the urban and rural populations discussed later in this chapter, and it pledges to make the solution its top priority. The CPC pledges to improve crop subsidies and keep agricultural prices at higher levels.

This is not to say that China will keep all its pledges and meet all its goals, but the Five-Year Plan gives us an insight into its thinking regarding what is important enough to be written in stone for the next five years.

The Great Migration: From Country to City

The astonishing economic successes described above could not have happened if not for another important essential ingredient—masses of people ready, willing, and able to do the work. In other words, cheap labor in abundance.

China has over 150 million migrant workers who have moved from the country areas into the urban, industrialized areas. This is already the largest migration in the history of the world. It is the equivalent of creating another country with a work force the size of the U.S. work force in a period of just a few years. The majority of total migration has been in the last six years.

Migration has affected the culture of the country. It has led to better education, more equality for women, and an impact on many more areas of Chinese life. The full impact of migration has only begun to be felt. Without the existence of the vast labor pool and the social and economic factors that facilitated migration, the economic miracle of China would not have happened.

The story of the migration is essential to understanding how China's change of policy was translated so quickly and consistently into such robust growth.

China's system of household registration, which is needed for access to housing, education, and health care, still makes it extremely difficult to switch from rural to urban residence, although the government is finally starting to address that issue.

The estimated labor pool of surplus rural labor is officially estimated at 150 million, but China still has about 600 million people in rural areas, many of whom, if not considered surplus labor, can be called "underemployed" or "marginally employed." They could be added to the estimated surplus if an effort were made to free them by introducing some minimal labor-saving tools and equipment and policies.

The proportion of China's population living in towns and cities is rising markedly. It is now over 40 percent, up from 18 percent in 1978. This increase is accelerating and will accelerate more if the government institutes incentives to facilitate the move to towns and cities.

As stated earlier, the availability of China's pool of labor was the most important single factor enabling the great economic growth. Having a vast pool of underemployed, educated people who were accustomed to hard work and low wages made China ripe for such a phenomenon.

The implications of this migration are mind-boggling. Its ramifications reach to the very roots of Chinese traditional culture. In rural China, a family works its small farm together, eats its meals together in the same house, and often sleeps in one big bed together. As the effects of migration become more and more pervasive, many cultural changes are occurring.

Studies find that money—or stated another way, poverty—isn't the only reason why Chinese migrants are leaving home. Other reasons include seeing the world and learning new skills. Also, some seek adventure or just escape from the dullness of everyday rural life. Many rural families are allotted such small plots that the land can easily be cultivated by many fewer people, so there is nothing much to do at home.

Migrating is hard to do. To leave and return shows defeat and the migrant loses face, so most migrants persevere once they leave their homes. By striking out, they believe that they have the chance to change their fate. However, many people in poor jobs in poor factories think that to move is useless because they wouldn't be able to find better jobs.

Migrants are called *liudong renkou*, or "floating population," but a report issued by a Chinese-government study group stated that 87 percent left home for a promised job or because someone said they could help them find a job. Given their relational society, Chinese migrants rely on friends, relatives, neighbors, and other acquaintances for help. They are not vagrants. Once someone becomes established somewhere with a job, he helps others make the transition.

Current migrants are the upper class of rural society. They are better educated and younger than those who remain. A study by the Chinese Academy of Social Sciences found that 78 percent of female migrants from one area had a junior high school education, compared to 43 percent of the total female population.

Some rural migrants with a college education earn twice as much in a month as their rural families earn on the farm in a year. Some rural families want someone in the family to be upwardly mobile, and they will sacrifice in order that one child can attend college.

Many migrants become lost from their families for a while after leaving home, and don't make contact again until they have a stable job. Migrants do a lot of job-hopping, and most don't stay in a job for a whole year. They are hired with a six-month minimum agreement.

Many migrants will work for a period of years, live frugally, and send home every spare dollar. The money that they send home is already the greatest source of wealth in rural China, a source larger than the farm income. Finally, they feel they have earned their freedom, and they begin to work for themselves and plan families.

The Income Gap

Unlike in the United States, where the average farm is about 500 acres, China's family farms typically consist of four to six acres. An individual is typically assigned one to two acres. With that little to work with, there isn't much potential for rural workers to increase their income. In order to bridge the income gap between rural and urban populations, farm income must increase, which means that the average acreage per worker must increase and rural productivity must rise. Average urban income, which was much higher to begin with, has about tripled in the last decade, while rural income has less than doubled from the lower base.

Economic disparities between rural and urban areas and between coastal and interior regions have already fueled some resentment among segments of the Chinese populace.

Coastal cities have been much more aggressive in seeking economic progress. This can be attributed mostly to local officials, since much of China's policymaking is very decentralized. There are many large cities by U.S. standards that are relatively untouched by the economic boom, places where wages are substantially lower than the average wages in the better-known urban areas where the local governments have been trying to encourage foreign investment.

These interior cities are now under a great deal of pressure to encourage foreign investment and institute policies that are starting to result in significant economic advances. Chongqing, for example, with a population of 3.4 million people, has an average wage of only $125 per month. The local government, through accommodative actions, has attracted Ford Motor Company to open operations in Chongqing, where it can take advantage of the low wages.

Many other interior cities now realize that their low wages attract investment money, and they are becoming much more solicitous and cooperative with companies that may invest or locate in these regions. Local government cooperation can result in concessions of real value.

There are many reasons to consider inland areas. First, there are major cost benefits in labor as compared to more popular coastal cities—perhaps as much as 40 percent—and in land cost, as much as 70 percent. Also, the local governments may be more appreciative of your investment, which may result in concessions.

Many inland cities are making major investments in infrastructure, with money from both the central and provincial governments. This allows inland cities to connect to coastal ports via multilane highways and other improvements.

The interior is growing at perhaps a 12 percent to 15 percent rate as compared to China's overall 9 percent. Also, China is developing consumer spending in the interior to make it more attractive for workers and companies and to balance trade growth with consumerism. Wal-Mart and KFC, for example, have recognized the opportunities and are growing quickly in the interior.

The problem with obtaining economic advances in rural areas is that the government must maintain the illusion of full employment or nearly full employment, but it must help rural people move into the mainstream of the country's progress if it is to bridge the earnings gap and allay rural discontent. At present, farmers only lease their land. They do not own it, so they can't sell it for a stake to use to move to cities.

As people move from rural areas, the amount of cultivatable land per worker increases somewhat, but eventually, the government will have to come up with a plan to allow and perhaps encourage the migration, or at least to free enough new workers to fuel China's future economic growth. That plan should also seek to create a modern, efficient farming system for the long term.

The government is trying to close the widening income gap between rich and poor and urban and rural people.

Some officials have already spoken out, warning that the gap would eventually cause popular unrest, something Beijing wants to avoid at all costs. To squelch turbulence, China has announced some action plans and has held public hearings on the subject.

While Beijing realizes the importance of urbanizing its population, its policies as yet do not fully reflect that aim.

Private Property

China is firmly on the road to capitalism, judging by its recent policy changes in the area of private versus public ownership of businesses and real property. Recent policy decisions include, first, the recognition that state-owned businesses are not as efficient (or as profitable) as private companies and, second, the realization that private land ownership builds wealth for the country and a much larger tax base.

There is now a strong and effective effort to convert state businesses to primarily privately owned enterprises. At the same time, rules on foreign ownership have been drastically eased, allowing FOEs (Foreign Owned Enterprises) to purchase interests in some state businesses.

Often the government retains a minority interest in important enterprises that are private, but the aim is to make them private stockholder-owned businesses. Because the state has owned all property and other natural resources, as well as monopolies and many of the largest firms in key industries, China has huge potential to turn these assets into financial wealth for its citizens.

Every first-tier nation in the world has private-property rights. Since the government has recognized that one of the keys to wealth-building is giving individuals the right to own real property, it now will allow private ownership of property with the same rights as public property. That removes one of the last impediments to China's becoming one of the wealthiest countries on earth.

Regarding real property, China is in the process of changing private-property laws so that individuals and companies may own property with the same rights as state-owned property. That is to say, individuals and companies can have true ownership including title, and transferability, as opposed to the leasing of property where the title remained with the government. This is of great significance to the process of accumulating wealth in China. It will provide market value to real property, allowing for collateralizing of loans and investment alternatives.

Even while making changes to lead China on a course that will dramatically upgrade economic conditions, Beijing has not changed its political positions. The government has added businesspeople to its council, but everyone is still appointed, not elected.

The new attitude toward private ownership of businesses and real property will have many ramifications, which are discussed in some detail throughout this book. One of these ramifications is China's need for Chinese brand recognition, which Beijing now understands. The Chinese recognize, just as the Japanese did some years before, that building brand identity and loyalty is the best way to maximize revenue. In the early stages of industrializing, the focus was on quantity, but Beijing now realizes that along with brand recognition, long-term success requires increased emphasis on technological, design, and quality improvements, as well as the necessary advertising skills and experience.

The Chinese are now taking steps to gain world recognition for Chinese-branded products. Chinese companies are also testing the waters now to try to arrange sales of Chinese brands directly to American retailers. For example, Haier has recently made some marketing progress in the United States, selling its own brand through Target and other retailers. Lenovo (formerly Legend Group Ltd.), the Chinese computer company that bought IBM's personal computer business, is now selling computers under its own brand in the United States. We might even expect a Chinese car marketed here in the next few years.

Another ramification is the creation of larger companies in many fields as large, formerly state-owned companies become private. This has several major implications. There will be more public stock ownership as larger companies go public, and there will be more merger and acquisition activity as larger companies with more assets, borrowing power, and/or public stock seek to grow by that route. This will increase the concentration of market share in fewer hands.

Another consequence is that more companies will be professionally managed and there will be more demand for professional Chinese managers, which will inevitably push middle management wages higher.

The country and many of its largest companies recognize the need for in-house talent able to deal with the explosion of internationalism in China. They need people skilled in dealing with foreigners, and if they are to market their goods internationally they need to know how to deal with the international regulatory and compliance situations that they will face.

One Chinese habit is denying facts by explaining why they could not be true. With international competition, this will no longer be possible. The larger Chinese companies are learning that international competition is a lot tougher than the domestic competition they have faced in the past. In 2005, Dell won a computer contract at a Chinese government agency over the domestic favorite, Lenovo. The agency saw Lenovo's quality as slipping and its customer service as lacking. This was one of the motivations for Lenovo to buy IBM's PC business.

The playing field is still not level in most business areas, but it is becoming more so. Chinese buyers show much more pragmatism in their decisions than do their Japanese counterparts, who retain nationalistic attitudes. If domestic companies show themselves not to be on a par with foreign competitors, Chinese buyers are quicker to go for the practical. This will slow Chinese expansion on a global scale, since the companies must be competitive domestically before they can go global. To their credit, the Chinese have been allowing more and more free competition to occur in an effort to make their domestic companies competitive.

Government Programs and Development Incentives

The government gives and takes away incentives as it sees fit in order to achieve its current objectives. Once the goals change, whatever incentives they had offered can disappear and new ones can appear to meet new objectives. Some companies were in businesses that China deemed desirable and received duty-free and tax incentives for them to open operations there. Some opened and received the favorable treatment promised, but others that were slower acting saw the government's emphasis change, and proffered incentives dropped. Government incentives can be mercurial, with some here today and gone tomorrow. Others, though, are obviously long term. For example, the government wants to develop noncoastal areas, especially western China. In order to do that, it offers incentives such as favorable terms on land, as well as financial help for new facilities. If your business fits in western China or another inland environment, you might receive some major concessions.

The government's policy had been one of encouraging controlled development inland, while coastal provinces continued to grow uncontrolled on their own. That is completely changed now, and the Central Government is strongly supporting inland growth.

If you are interested in western China (Xinjiang Region, for example), keep in mind that it is not like the western United States versus the midwestern or eastern United States. If you are expecting western China to be like the rest of China, you are in for a culture shock. China is not as homogeneous as you might think. Western China is a world of its own. Most people in the Western world think of Xi'an as western China, but in fact, Xi'an is located roughly in the middle of China. The western half of China is west of Xi'an. Styles, customs, and even cultures are different in the western half. There are two cultures, two languages, and two lifestyles, side by side. Even the facial features of half the people are different.

The population density is far less than that of eastern China, and this area boasts some breathtaking scenery.

Despite the government's efforts to promote the region economically economic development still lags behind eastern China markedly, not only in absolute terms, but also in the rate of development. Government incentives for development will remain in western China for the foreseeable future.

Trade Agreements

China now sees that free trade is in its best interest, and the country has become a strong advocate of it. So far, it has succeeded in cutting its import tariffs to 9.4 percent, down from 15.3 percent in 2001. The government points to that statistic as proof that it is trying to level the playing field.

China is also very active in seeking regional economic cooperation with various countries and regions, and will deal with anyone, including enemies of the United States. Political convictions do not influence its trade decisions, at least not in favor of the United States. The key factor is whether trade will be economically favorable for China, without regard for world peace or other such factors. China does, however, see international trade as a tool to lessen American influence.

The Chinese government wants to import cheaper raw materials and consequently export price-advantaged finished goods in return. Toward that end, it is putting in place agreements with its neighbors and with Africa, South America, and many other areas previously neglected.

Africa now supplies almost 20 percent of U.S. oil imports, and is also a major supplier of raw materials to the United States. China is challenging us for these goods. China's trade with Africa nearly tripled to $30 billion in three years. In Asia, China now buys more than it sells to other Asian countries.

Inflation and Bank Lending

There have been many reports and much speculation recently about China's "overheated" economy. Most of these are pessimistic, dwelling on coming inflation and out-of-control bank lending, and the attempts of the central bank to tighten monetary policy. Beijing would like to rein in bank loans, specifically new loans to industries that it feels are growing too fast, such as steel, cars, cement, aluminum, and real estate.

The Chinese government has confirmed its own concern, and recently took action by increasing interest rates for the first time in forty years.

There have also been articles on the booming growth of the steel industry and its dominance in world production (doubled since 2000), which is threatening to glut the world supply. This is especially dangerous if the boom in China slows and the output is thrown onto the world market. Right now, China is using most of its own production for internal growth in the industrial, commercial, and housing areas.

China now consumes twice as much steel as does the United States, even though its economy is only one-eighth the size, and yet China has become a net exporter of steel. Much of this has occurred because local officials granted and encouraged these mills in order to foster local growth. Now, the Central Government is discouraging the start of work on any more steel mills.

Loose lending practices have been a causal factor in the proliferation of steel mills. There is now a shortage of electricity and iron ore to supply these mills. Although the mills use down time when electricity is not available to do maintenance work, China could soon have more manufacturing capacity than available power supply and raw materials support.

Regarding bank lending policies, one anecdote tells of a reporter interviewing senior officials of major banks, who had to look through their papers to answer the question, "How high are Chinese interest rates?" Enforcing the dictates of the central bank and the government to curb new loans to sectors that officials believe are growing too fast may prove difficult, because the Chinese financial system is not able to allocate capital efficiently. The government is now considering tougher enforcement of capital controls, such as cracking down on the illegal ways in which banks conspire with their customers to dodge restrictions on bringing in speculative capital.

It is true that there are many non-performing loans and that the banking industry needs much more regulation and supervision. However, the government realizes that the banking industry must be made whole with no loss of money to any depositor, or the failure of any bank. It will do that by buying the non-performing loans and reselling them. The government is absolutely committed to this policy.

The issue of how to exert more control is more complex. There is de facto decentralization of the banking processes. That fact, together with China's relationship-oriented way of doing business, makes it especially difficult for banking officials to obey the regulations in an impersonal manner. Some graft has occurred, but the whole tradition of courtesy and personal relationships presents the larger problem. Bank officials can't say no to a friend. Eventually, though, the government will likely get enough procedural rules in place (and enforced) to allow banking officials to give a courteous and cogent explanation to friends as to why they are prevented from granting personal requests.

Economic Concerns

It is not clear whether China will be able to control growth, interest rates, etc., but comparisons have been made to the economic downturn in Asia in the early 1990s. The inflation rate and other numbers were higher and the feeling is that China's condition now is not as fragile as the East Asia economies in 1993–94.

This whole discussion overlooks two very important factors that make comparisons with U.S. economic history not directly relevant. American business is driven mainly by the American consumer. China is producing in large part for foreign consumers. The export business has become a major portion of the Chinese economy. This business will only be impacted if there is a worldwide recession or if new manufacturing orders are diverted elsewhere.

China's underpinnings are not only the solidly growing domestic consumer market, but also other world markets. The trend is firmly set. China's share of the world's manufacturing will increase in the near future. If an industry that produces mainly for domestic consumption such as the steel industry overheats, it is not the major element driving the economy. Furthermore, steel prices have recently risen very dramatically. They will have to accept the realities of the free market and roll back some of these increases and curb some of the more inefficient production, but these issues will have a minor impact on the overall economy.

Inflation

Another current issue is whether or not, or the extent to which, China will have inflation. In China, inflation has more to do with definitions and statistics-gathering than with the real inflation that crops up from time to time in the United States.

Statistics in the United States are mature, comprising the same statistics gathered in the same way, which allow for reasonable comparison from period to period. In China, statistics-gathering and the elements that make up final price are changing to some extent. Final consumer prices do not take into account certain changes in the elements that comprise the prices. China's distribution pattern, timeliness, display, and packaging are improving, meaning that more service is built into the price of the product.

Products that gave Chinese consumers few choices are in the process of differentiating themselves. The consumer is being treated to more product services with their purchases, with the cost of these services buried in the final price of the product. There is now more selection, more in-stock incidence, better displays, better packaging, and better service.

This consumer revolution makes price comparisons this period to last period or this period to the same period last year somewhat misleading. As differentiation continues to succeed and build consumer preferences, prices tend to rise. Real inflation is still very low, and Beijing is ready, willing, and able to act effectively.

Currency Revaluation

Another urgent issue is China's currency, as the *yuan* (pronounced "yuen," not "yu-ann"), is under a great deal of pressure to be revalued. China has built Foreign Exchange Reserves of over $500 billion. There has been and still is a great deal of pressure being brought by the United States and others for Beijing to revalue China's currency. In 2005, China revalued its currency by less than 2 percent. (The *Wall Street Journal* suggested that the Chinese currency be called the "yawn" because of the minimal revaluation as opposed to what was demanded and expected.)

This has not satisfied most critics. China fixed the yuan to the dollar about twelve years ago, making for a very stable currency. This has allowed China to enjoy tremendous economic growth these past years, without any attendant currency instability. China shows every sign of resisting a precipitous further revaluation, which should allow its continued economic growth.

Legal Issues and Legislation

China never had a complete body of law addressing every facet of the economy, or even most facets of the economy. Since its new economic epiphany, and more particularly since its entry into the WTO, China has been frantically passing new rules and regulations, trying to bring its laws into the twenty-first century on all fronts at the same time. From 2001 to now, China has amended more than 2,000 laws and regulations, and abolished more than 800 others.

Needless to say, the Chinese government has a daunting task. Progress has been uneven, with some areas being addressed while related areas are not. Overall, though, China has done a remarkably good job, considering the size and complexity of the task.

China already has laws banning many fraudulent practices that bilk consumers, and many additional decrees are being passed, such as a ban on false or misleading claims made in television advertisements. The State Administration for Industry and Commerce (SAIC), the country's top advertising industry regulator, has recently been very active in pushing such decrees. However, China's increasing flow of anti-fraud and other protective laws cannot be effective unless the country puts into place a strong, dedicated, and sustained law-enforcement push, which has not yet happened.

In the next few years China will most likely pass anti-monopoly laws, as it now realizes that some large multinational firms control dominant positions in the Chinese market.

On the other hand, China turns a blind eye to collusion under the buddy system. If you are involved in a business that is dominated by a few Chinese firms, you may want to test the waters to make sure you can get beneficial treatment. No investment can rely on verbal promises alone. Get concrete proof that you can get what you want. The enabling part is that the colluders will accept foreigners into the group if it's in their economic interest.

Part Two

Issues and Problems

In this section of the book, we'll address the major barriers to successful dealings in China. The first three chapters here deal with areas of difficulty that should come as no surprise: language, culture, and customs.

Language differences will be a constant problem, and we'll address them in a couple of ways in Chapter 3: first, a very brief discussion of the Chinese language itself, to help you to understand something about it and to learn how to pull out some key phrases on your own; and second, a discussion of how to get the right kind of help in translation. (Of course, that level of knowledge is just for goodwill, and is not a substitute for actual communication.) Chapter 4 discusses in detail the cultural issues that you will be facing, and how and why those issues will be important in reaching long-standing agreements. Chinese customs are taken up in even more detail in Chapter 5, including the best advice on how to avoid insulting your Chinese associates and how to build personal relationships in China. The chapter ends with a very important word on the dangers of assumptions.

In Chapters 6, 7, and 8 of Part Two, we'll deal with the important areas of financial and legal issues, travel and daily life, and import/export concerns.

Chapter 3

Language and Translation

No MATTER HOW GOOD you are at languages, unless you have a big head start, you will need a translator. Do not underestimate the size of the language barrier you will need to overcome in China.

Communications is one of the biggest problems facing any organization. Many books and articles have been written and speeches and courses given on the subject of communications difficulties among people who have the same culture and speak the same language. How much more difficult is it for people from different cultures, speaking different languages, to communicate effectively?

Chinese versus English

English is a very direct and precise language, with words expressing many nuances and degrees of the same basic thought. You can be surprised, amazed, astounded, or dumbfounded, depending on how surprised you really were. Each degree can be expressed by a different word.

Chinese is less precise. As a matter of fact, the Chinese don't see the point of making up new words to express shades of difference. Their language often combines common words for a more precise meaning. For example, the Chinese word for "saliva" means "mouth-water." The Chinese argue that this method is easier and completely understandable, and that it is unnecessary to make up a different word.

When people refer to the Chinese language, they generally mean the Mandarin dialect, which is the official dialect of China. (Incidentally, the official language of Taiwan is also Mandarin.) Different areas of China have their own regional dialects, but the great majority of businesspeople speak Mandarin as well as their local dialect. Your interpreter will need to communicate in Mandarin, because very few of the Chinese people speak workable English.

In China, dialects are, for all intents and purposes, separate languages, because a speaker of one dialect cannot understand another. However, the Chinese dialects all have a common written language that the speakers of each dialect understand, so while your interpreter may not be able to communicate verbally with someone who does not speak Mandarin, he would be able to communicate in writing.

Americans find Chinese one of the most difficult languages to learn. There are several reasons for this. First, the Chinese language does not use an English alphabet. The Chinese do not use letters to spell words, but have different symbols for each separate sound.

The official translation of sounds into English alphabet characters is diabolically difficult, since neither vowels nor consonants are pronounced the same as they are in English. Even memorizing words is difficult, partly because no translations have the same meanings or roots as the corresponding words in English, so there are no roots that we already know that will help us with the meaning.

Also, word memorization must be more than just the sounds; it also involves tones. The Chinese language utilizes mostly single-syllable words, so words are shorter, and many sound the same, with only the tone to distinguish the meaning. There are four basic tones: flat tone, voice rising, voice falling then rising, and voice falling. It is said that Chinese is the only language requiring both sides of the brain, a result of the dependence on tones as well as sounds.

The Chinese people will be honored and appreciative of any interest and knowledge you have of their language and customs, so you might like to start learning a few helpful phrases from Appendix 3. You will find helpful words and phrases along with the Chinese translation.

The standard Pinyin spelling of words using English characters is very confusing to Americans, so in addition to giving you the standard Pinyin spelling, the third column in the appendix is the best approximation of each word's pronunciation using English spelling.

The Importance of a Good Translator

If you do not already speak Chinese, your communications with the Chinese people will be dependent on your translator. There are many stories of near and real disasters caused by poor translators.

At a dinner between top executives of a large American company and a major potential Chinese partner, everyone had drunk a prodigious amount of alcohol. At a meeting the next morning, the Chinese host tried to convey his admiration for people who could put away that much alcohol without being obviously affected. However, his translator translated his statement to the group as, "You drink too much."

Before major damage could be done, one of the American group, with a better command of both languages, interjected the true intended meaning of the comment, with an explanation, thus averting a potentially dangerous situation of innocent misunderstanding.

That's the kind of translator you need for serious business—one who interprets underlying meanings, connotations, and feelings, not someone who just translates words. Your translator needs to comprehend your intentions and the intentions of the people you're communicating with and then help to get the thoughts and intentions of each across to the other.

Good translators are hard to find. This is not an area that can be compromised. You will have a tough enough job coming to a meeting of minds, given the differences in culture, customs, and practices, without having additional misunderstandings in language.

Keep in mind that jokes are especially difficult to translate. Even people who share the same language and culture often don't understand, or worse, misinterpret someone else's humor.

One of my firm's clients told a joke in China that Chinese-Americans had found very funny. The other party's interpreter completely missed the point and the humor. The expressions of the listeners were grim, since the way the joke was interpreted made it sound as though it was in very bad taste. We tried to tell them how treacherous and ambiguous the words were to translate, joked with their interpreter to try to save his face, then retold the joke, which they found very funny the second time around.

When speaking to the Chinese, even to your interpreter, speak slowly, distinctly, and use the most common words you can think of to express ideas. Even the better interpreters don't fully understand most American idioms, so try to listen to yourself and substitute common language for idioms.

Don't trust your host's translator. This is one of the most common errors made by Americans inexperienced in China. You may get a really good translator, but most in-house translators would not even pass for fair. Also, they are not so comfortable with the language that they can devote some of their attention to trying to understand your mood and underlying intent. If you want to conclude any serious agreement, select your own interpreter and let that person communicate for you. It is a great aid, and not just a duplication of effort.

Understanding Numbers

If you are trying to communicate the concept of large numbers with the Chinese, you will need to understand that their whole numbering concept is different (although it is a decimal system just as ours is). Luckily, this only gets confusing when communicating large numbers.

The American numbering notation breaks at every three places. We mark our place with a comma. One thousand is expressed as "1,000." Then we do not use a different word for a number until a million, expressed as "1,000,000," which is three more digits and another comma. The same is true for each larger concept, such as billion or trillion.

In contrast, the Chinese numbering notation breaks at every four places. Therefore, the Chinese have a separate word for 10,000, which is *wan* (pronounced "wen"). While Americans think of 10,000 as ten 1,000s, the Chinese think of it as one 10,000—*wan*.

If Americans are trying to express a million (1,000,000), the Chinese think of it as one hundred 10,000s. Their next conceptual number break is four digits more than ten thousand (10,000), which is 100 million (100,000,000). The Chinese call 100 million *yi* (pronounced "yee").

When communicating large numbers, write down the digits instead of communicating verbally. You can write numbers in sequence with commas, the way you normally would, but it would be more helpful to write the numbers without commas, so your Chinese counterparts can group them in fours more easily.

Chapter 4

Culture: Ancient and New

MANY OF THE PAST TRUISMS about Chinese culture are in a state of flux, as several factors have converged to begin changing long-standing traditions. Many of these changes are counter to Confucian teaching. Many are still evolving. Therefore, the future of the Chinese culture has not been formed yet.

There is a generation gap in culture, with the traditions discussed in this chapter being the main customs and those fully accepted by the older generations.

There are four main factors that are changing traditional Chinese Confucian culture and affecting the values of the younger generations. They are:

- The one-child rule
- The migration of people from rural to urban areas
- Economic growth
- The 36 Strategies

The one-child rule (which is explained below in the section called "Deference to Age, and the Younger Generation") has changed the relationships within families and dramatically altered the way children are brought up, raising the relative importance of children within the family and increasing the relative value of the individual to the family.

If there is only one child in each family and that child is a girl, the result is that girls become better educated and have a greater feeling of self-worth, thus improving the general status of women in society.

The migration of people from the country to the cities has changed not only living patterns and economic factors, but also family relationships. Migration has led to some rural young people pursuing better education in order to get a better job. If they succeed, they make much more money and are more worldly than the older members of the family, causing the younger generation to challenge or lose respect for elders, and changing traditional family values.

The dramatic economic growth has increased the emphasis on material values, raised the image of business, and made people more materialistic, cosmopolitan, and independent. More young people are opting for independence. For example, the more wealthy choose to care for their parents outside their home, by buying them an apartment or putting them in a nursing home, rather than living together as an extended family.

The trend toward individualism has caused other changes in family patterns. Divorce, which was taboo not too many years ago, has grown dramatically. While not nearly at America's level yet, it is not uncommon now and is growing at a rate of 20 percent each year.

This book points out many customs and cultural behaviors, without going much into China's cultural history. One key point bears mention, though. Americans are somewhat familiar with *Sun Tzu's Art of War*, but few have heard of the 36 Strategies, which have changed many customs and behavior patterns in China. Though unfamiliar to foreigners, the Strategies are taught in junior high school in China and are widely known there.

The 36 Strategies are derived from old proverbs, sayings, and stories. They most likely date from the 1600s, during the late Ming Dynasty. The Strategies were actually forgotten for many years until an old reprint of them was discovered in the early 1940s; they then gained popularity with the Communists and have since become common wisdom in China.

The Strategies represent a complete departure from Confucianism and its code of honor. Many Americans still believe that Chinese culture is based on Confucianism, but the philosophy of the 36 Strategies is to win at any cost. According to the Strategies, winning is everything, and it should be obtained by any means that will succeed. Each Strategy illustrates how to employ particular tactics of deceit, treachery, and ruthlessness.

These tactics have succeeded in business, politics, and war in modern China, and they explain many of the actions and difficulties you will face in doing business there. Americans are inculcated with a particular concept of fairness and honor, and we often think that everyone else has our values. We believe that people are what they say they are and what they appear to be. The 36 Strategies actually teach the Chinese to use our beliefs as a weapon against us. As an American doing business in China, you would gain much insight by reading the specifics of the 36 Strategies.

When considering the traditional Chinese values discussed in this section, be mindful of all the changes in values (such as the 36 Strategies) that are taking place as well. It's also important for you to comprehend the substantive differences in the American and Chinese cultures if you are to have a real chance to reach a meeting of the minds. The American culture is confrontational, whereas Chinese culture is cooperative. Western culture tries to conquer, but the Chinese are trained to accept things—at least outwardly. The Chinese stress stability and group cohesion. The group is more important than the individual.

The Importance of Relationships

Here in America, we appreciate the value of contacts. However, in China, the value of relationships is far greater and is ingrained in the culture. It cannot be overestimated. China is a relationship-oriented society. Much of what is accomplished or not accomplished is based on who you know and how close your relationship is.

The Chinese call it *guanxi* (pronounced "gwentsee"). In business, it is the network and interaction of your relationships. It is based on regular, friendly contact and exchange of favors.

Even the way the Chinese maintain their relationships is much more intense. Through the years, they literally keep in touch with friends going all the way back to elementary school. Most Chinese people can number among their contacts hundreds of people, male and female, whom they have met or spoken to by phone in the last year.

In contrast, when you go to an American reunion of any kind, you can probably count on your fingers the number of people with whom you have been in contact since the last reunion.

Chinese think in terms of relationships when they seek information, jobs, or favors, and they are not often disappointed. Having relationships carries prestige and weight.

As a foreigner, you may not be able to have that extensive a network in China, but you should start building your Chinese network upon your first contact. Maintain it and add to it. A web of strong personal relationships will help ensure smoother development of business in China, as well as all kinds of other advantages.

The Value of Hierarchy and Saving Face

Chinese culture has difficulty accepting equality. It understands hierarchy better—the concept of the superior and the inferior.

The Chinese feel much more comfortable when they know your organizational authority structure. Preparing at least a basic organizational chart for them is a good idea.

You are probably also aware of the importance of "face" in Asia. That is true of China. Several manifestations of this characteristic will affect you. If the Chinese don't know something, they rarely say "I don't know." So, if you ask a question for which you think they know the answer and they don't, they will respond with their best guess. The danger here is that you will take what they say as factual when it is not.

Also, if there is an important point you are trying to make that must be understood, don't assume that just because people are nodding their heads and seem to be agreeing that they really understand. To discover whether they really do know or understand key points, ask oblique questions that will let you know the depth of their understanding. Don't directly challenge them, though, or they lose face.

The Chinese will say "I'm sorry" for little accidents or accidents of fate, but not mistakes of their judgment. If they bump into you, or spill something, they will say *duei bu chi* (pronounced "dway boo chee," and meaning "I'm sorry"); if they wrongly estimated a cost or a price, however, they will give you their reasons why it happened, but they won't apologize. Don't expect them to use words like "I was wrong." Don't take this personally. Their culture doesn't permit it.

Sometimes the Chinese will apologize in other, nonverbal ways, such as giving a gift or performing a favor, shortly after the incident.

Making Sure You Are Understood

Another way in which their reluctance to admit a lack of understanding will affect you is with your translator. Unless the translator was brought up in the American culture, he will tend not to ask you questions if he doesn't understand something. He will attempt to translate your statements anyway, sometimes with disastrous results. Talk with your interpreter about this. If he is the other person's interpreter, assume that this is his tendency.

To question your interpreter's understanding on any point, independently confirm that he understands what you said. Ask him to explain to you what you said in his own words.

In any case, these cultural differences make it easier for the Chinese to unquestioningly accept non sequiturs than it is for Americans, which can lead to greater misunderstanding.

Understanding "Yes" and "No"

Here's another cultural point that will be meaningful in negotiating. The Chinese have a word for "yes," but not for "no." Their words for "no" mean "not yes."

If they mean "no," they may say the equivalent of "maybe." That usually means "no," especially with the older generation. "Yes" often means "maybe," depending on the supporting context. If your interpreter is very good, ask him what his read is on the underlying intent of the answer. If you are trying to interpret the answer yourself, gauge the enthusiasm with which it was said.

Deference to Age, and the Younger Generation

Chinese show deference to older members of the family. In stating their names, the last name is first, designating the importance of family as the primary identity over the individual. This tradition is one of the oldest, but it is now being severely challenged by the migration factor and other events.

In an urban environment, children work longer hours and are more devoted to their jobs and to making money than their parents were. Consequently, they have less time for their parents.

In the rural environment the elders, usually men, make the family decisions. The elder children discipline the younger ones, and the younger children obey their elders.

What is happening is that when the children migrate and get situated in a job, they earn much more than does the family back on the land. This gives the children a sense of superiority, and the family loses some control over them. These children are independent at an earlier age, and they learn to do things for themselves without deference to their elders. (In raising children, the Chinese try to make a child dependent on the family, while Americans try to make a child independent.)

Eventually, many migrants experience alienation from their rural home and feel more comfortable in the urban environment. These feelings are changing some family values and creating more family stress.

China's drastic one-child-rule solution to the population problem has many implications for the generation that will someday be assuming power. In 1979, when China's population explosion seemed to be out of control, the government, under then-leader Deng Xioping, mandated the one-child rule, which said that all urban couples could only have one child. The original rule was later moderated. Now, in the countryside, if the first child is a girl, the parents can have a second child; and in urban areas, if both parents are the product of the one-child limitation, they may have two children.

Because of this law, younger Chinese people, having received more attention and sense of importance in the family, are more assertive. Also, the attainment of individual wealth is having an effect on culture. While for the most part the traditional Chinese culture remains intact with older people, many in the younger generation are challenging tradition. Changes are definitely in progress.

The historic reason for having more children is for help on the land. This need has diminished as modern farming techniques have taken hold. That, along with the one-child rule, has pretty much met the objective of controlling China's exploding population growth.

Another ramification of the one-child rule that is starting to affect the Chinese economic landscape is the fact that with one child only, the family has more disposable income, and the child has six potential sources of income, including the parents and both sets of grandparents. This is affecting buying patterns markedly, making younger people a much more important market segment.

Among the younger generation there is definitely what we refer to as a "rat race," Chinese style. There is also a subtle but definitely major change in allegiances from birth family to marriage family.

An interesting survey pertaining to younger people's living patterns shows that some 30 percent of urban children twenty to thirty years old, even married couples, are still living with their parents.

Another interesting note about education of the younger generation is that Chinese children have not been taught very much about the history of World War II. They don't know that America had anything to do with the Japanese leaving China. They think the Chinese army forced the Japanese out.

Decision-Making

The Asian tradition of slow decision-making is due in part to the people's group orientation. Many people feel obligated to get the family involved in important decisions, even if they are certain of the outcome.

However, entrepreneurs with considerable capital, self-confidence, and assertiveness have arisen in the last few years. They are not afraid to make their own decisions quickly, and without consultation.

If such people give you the answer that you are seeking, make sure to explain to them in detail (and later in writing) what their agreement entails. Spell out their obligation. (For more on this, see Chapter 13, which explains the art of negotiating.)

Deadlines

You should also understand that the Chinese concept of time is different from that of Americans. Chinese people do not want to be rushed. If you insist on quick decisions, you will be disappointed with the result. They usually view a time deadline as a loose target date, not as a commitment of honor. They may be thinking that the accepted deadline may be met if everything falls into place without a problem. Remember that most of their business experiences are with fellow Chinese businessmen, who are very tolerant of missed deadlines.

If you operate on the "just in time" method of management, or if missing a deadline will have severe consequences in any other way, you must explain the consequences of missing this deadline as opposed to a soft deadline, to the point that you are sure they understand the stakes. Some firms have learned to incorporate penalties for missed deadlines into contracts.

Patience

Most people attribute infinite patience to the Chinese. In many ways they are very patient, especially the older generation. They will work hard toward a deeply desired goal and will put up with great hardships along the way. Unfortunately, this is not true for minor or intermediate business goals. On the contrary, when it comes to business goals, they do not want to wait very long for rewards, and they do not like to take long-term risks. It's possible to change their reluctance to defer rewards, but only if they are thoroughly convinced that payday will come, and that it is definitely in their best interest to wait.

The Chinese people do have a deserved reputation for loving to gamble, but they have an aversion to gambling in business. They have a heightened ability to compartmentalize issues: gambling is entertainment, whereas business is business.

Empathy and Gratitude

We have covered some crucial differences between the Chinese culture and our own, with the understanding that culture shapes the way people think, their values, their way of looking at the world, the decisions they make, and the things they do.

In trying to comprehend the Chinese culture and how it relates to our own, there is one observation that explains many anomalies. Most Chinese people do certain things that Westerners feel is rude or selfish, which is counter to other actions you may have observed in their behavior. The Chinese are basically a gentle, kind, and generous people, but some of their actions and decisions do seem out of character.

Americans have a very diverse culture. In order to succeed at almost anything, we must learn to relate to diverse peoples, to get inside other people's minds, think like they think, know their perspective, walk a mile in their moccasins. In short, we are taught empathy.

The Chinese are taught almost the opposite. They are taught to respect the privacy of other people. Most older people have had some experience with living in very close proximity with other families, sometimes in the same room, where they learned to block out the activities and the very presence of other people.

It is not surprising, then, that empathy is not highly developed there. They often don't try to understand things from other people's perspectives. If they seem to disregard what you want, they are not doing this to be intentionally rude or unresponsive. They are just not considering you at all, since they have learned to block out other people sometimes.

You also will likely find that the Chinese have no more understanding of "gratitude" than they do of "empathy." They are pragmatic. They will repay a favor if it is in their best interest to do so. They will not repay a favor if it is not in their long-term interest.

What makes this dangerous ground is that the Chinese are very adept at displaying the trappings that we hope to see without necessarily feeling the underlying emotion that we associate with particular actions or words. Many times Chinese people may express how grateful they are that you have done them a favor, taught them something, or given them an opportunity that was not clearly earned. They can repeat their thanks with the utmost expressions of sincerity and even bow to emphasize their gratitude. You will see what a surface emotion this is when any disagreement arises, or when it is their turn to return the favor.

It is generally pragmatism, not gratitude, that rules their actions.

Posturing

Many of the Chinese are great character actors. They can play on any perceived emotions that will get them what they want. They can appear subservient and helpless, then change quickly to being imperious, and then to perfectly cooperative, depending upon the circumstances, and display no guilt afterward. In such cases, they do not judge their actions by any ethical or moral standards—only by the results.

Americans usually do judge themselves on ethical and moral standards. Our history is not perfect, but today most Americans give others the benefit of the doubt. It can be one of our fatal flaws. By the time we learn that the other guy did not deserve the benefit of the doubt, it is too late. We have been taken. Do not give people the benefit of the doubt if they haven't earned it, and if they won't give you the same. Why trust someone who doesn't trust you?

Many of the Chinese know how to play to the weaknesses in an American's typical approach. They will make you feel appreciated and respected, but in dealing with them, bear in mind that these manifestations on their part may not be heartfelt. Always be cautious and always protect yourself. At the same time, don't be cynical.

The Attraction of Western Culture

Many young people in China want to emulate the American lifestyle and Western culture. Culturally, the Chinese people have embraced Western pop culture—movies, music, fashion, fads, and so on. Many middle-class families use English names. Many people believe that China's traditions have not kept pace with the changing times.

Western entertainment is making big inroads into mainland China. Western movies have been big hits in China for some years now. Even Broadway has noticed China and is tapping that emerging market for Western culture. The musical *The Phantom of the Opera* played at the Shanghai Grand Theatre in 2005 to a virtually sold-out audience for a three-month run and brought in $8 million in tickct sales at an average ticket price of about $40.

For clues as to how American culture plays in China, many people are carefully watching the new Hong Kong Disneyland, which opened in September 2005.

Gender Roles and Sex Discrimination

China is not a completely male-dominated society without opportunities for women as some cultures are, but in most jobs it is more difficult for a woman to succeed than it is for a man, and there is significant wage discrimination.

A sidelight is that children are in some ways less a consideration in China than in the United States. Women do not feel guilty about leaving their children in the hands of others, since they themselves were probably left in the hands of others. Chinese women have access to day-care centers at very low cost. Many rely on their parents or in-laws, and those who are successful enough hire an outsider. China is becoming a latchkey society.

There are some powerful female executives in the upper echelons of business in China now, but they are a definite exception. The CEO of the largest Chinese steel company is a woman, and there are many female entrepreneurs. It is easier for a woman to succeed big by starting a company than by climbing the executive ladder in an existing one.

China is trying to encourage its industries to give more opportunity to women, but as yet this intent does not carry enforced penalties. The one-child rule has helped greatly, though. If a family's only child is a daughter, they try to give her every advantage that they would have given a son, including higher education and even postgraduate work, which makes it easier for the women to compete for higher-level jobs.

Chapter 5

Customs: Food, Behavior, and Beliefs

CHINA HAS THE WORLD'S most varied cuisine. There are no food taboos, or preconceptions, so anything goes. As an American, though, you may not like to eat something that's staring back at you, or other creatures or flora that you are conditioned not to eat, such as insects, reptiles, flowers, roots, and so on.

Even after you rule out dishes because they are psychologically distasteful, you will find that there are many things you can enjoy. Every area has a different cuisine, so each time you go to a new city, try the local favorites. Along with providing a possible delightful experience, your efforts will please your hosts.

There are some distinct differences in tastes. Many Chinese people don't like common American foods. Close to 100 percent of Americans like ice cream, but many of the Chinese do not. Many Chinese people do not like a charcoal-broiled steak. Likewise, there are many Chinese foods that you won't like, even if they are not psychologically distasteful. For example, most Americans don't like Chinese bakery products. They look fine, but most taste bland by American standards.

If you get tired of Chinese food, and you would like to taste something similar to American food again, there are several American fast-food chains that are well established in China. McDonald's, KFC (remade into a hamburger place in the style of McDonald's), Subway, and Pizza Hut are a few of the more prominent ones. There are also some Chinese-run and American-run restaurants serving Western-type food that are pretty good. Ask your hotel for recommendations.

In eating Western-style food, even from American-owned chains, expect differences from the menus that you're used to in America. The most successful chains have adapted their foods to Chinese tastes. Also, the posted menus are in Chinese and the cashiers don't speak English. Some have English menus. To ask for a menu in English, the phrase is *"Qing ke yi gei wo yinwe cai dan"* (pronounced "tsing keh yee gay wah kai dahn").

Dining and Business

Food has a high priority in deal-making. The Chinese use it to bond with others and to seal agreements already made, but be aware that they seldom discuss new business at the table. Eating is a social—not a business—function.

Going Out to Eat

You will be invited to restaurants, not to personal homes, and if it is a middle- to large-size group, your host will arrange a private room. Most of the nicer restaurants have private rooms, and if you are hosting a meal for others, seek to arrange one.

Most homes, even those of prosperous business owners, are small and lack conveniences. If you are invited to a home, take a gift, such as flowers or candy. Whenever you visit a private home, remove your shoes as soon as you step inside the door and put them where all the other shoes are. Your hosts will have slippers for you to use inside the house.

Almost always you will be taken to a restaurant to eat. It is customary for your host to pay. You may offer to pay, but do not insist. The Chinese people feel insulted if they don't pay. Tell them that you will return the favor when they visit you.

Karaoke

The Chinese love karaoke. If they take you to dinner, you have a good chance of being taken to a private room that has a karaoke system. They may know some American songs, like "Red River Valley." You should dust off your singing voice and do the best that you can with a few of the famous American songs that they like (mostly oldies), if you know them.

You can make a huge hit by singing a popular Chinese song. It will take some practice, but you will see that their reaction makes it more than worthwhile.

Dining Etiquette

At the dining table, the host usually sits facing the door and the guest of honor (you) sits at his right. Don't refuse any course. If you really don't like it, at least make it look like you have tried it by moving it around in your plate.

It's important that you learn to use chopsticks. If you don't know how, ask someone who knows, and practice before you go, and at least make an effort to use them when you are eating with Chinese people whose opinion you care about. Hold the bottom chopstick stationary against your ring finger or ring and middle fingers, and then move the top stick up and down with your index finger to open and close. (See Appendix 4 for more about eating with chopsticks.)

When eating rice, hold the bowl near your mouth and push the rice into your mouth with the chopsticks. When you are finished eating, leave something on the plate to show that you are full. It's an insult for the host to not provide more than enough food for his guests, so if you leave an empty plate, they will give you something more.

One note of etiquette is to cover your mouth when using a toothpick. Also, try not to blow your nose at the table, but if you must, turn away from everyone. The Chinese do not normally use handkerchiefs.

Once the meal is over, Chinese people do not linger. Be prepared to leave immediately after the meal is finished.

Chinese Cuisine Is Lean

Whatever you think about Chinese cuisine, you will find almost no obese people in China and only a small minority of people who are noticeably overweight. This is not a diet book and does not advocate going to China just to lose weight, but the Chinese do get the combinations of factors called for by our own dietitians: exercise in the form of walking, riding bicycles, and climbing stairs, along with more healthful foods and fewer junk foods.

However, this relatively healthy lifestyle is in the process of changing. The purchase of cars for personal use is proliferating, people have more income to spend on food and restaurants, more elevators and escalators are being used, and China is becoming more influenced by Western lifestyles. It is inevitable that with less exercise and more food, more people will be somewhat overweight. That assumption is already proving true. Although the proportion is still very small, some urban people are slightly overweight now, and that proportion can be expected to increase.

Drinks and Toasts

Few restaurants have ice. Few of the Chinese have cold drinks. Most people in China like their drinks at room temperature, or sometimes even warm. They believe that cold drinks are unhealthy. You might have to learn to sometimes drink room-temperature drinks. Few restaurants have diet sodas, either. Food markets or larger convenience stores usually have Diet Coke or Diet Sprite, at least in cans. Coke is more prevalent than Pepsi, but most supermarkets have Pepsi products as well. You will be served tea often, and without diet sweeteners. If you must have sweeteners, carry some with you. The Chinese drink their tea plain, but if you like, you can ask for lemon or sugar. If you're lucky, you will get it.

Chinese fruit juices are very good, and most Americans like them. This may be because they have fewer preservatives and taste fresher.

Most Chinese men like to drink alcoholic beverages, especially when out with honored guests. Tsingtao brand beer is the most popular beer in China. If you would like a beer, it would be taken well if you ordered Tsingtao by name, but better restaurants also have foreign beers, including American beers like Miller and Budweiser.

Your Chinese associates will make repeated toasts. If several people from a host company are present, each feels obligated to make a toast. If you are not a drinker, you've got some fancy footwork ahead of you, but there are ways to handle this situation. You might have a drinker accompany you, so that person can drink the alcoholic beverages, while you fill your glass with soda or water. A typical Chinese toast is *gam* (pronounced "gahm"), equivalent to something like "cheers." When the Chinese say *gambei* ("gahmbay"), it tends to mean "bottoms up," and is a more significant toast. You are expected to drain your glass. Don't put too much in your glass at any time, so that if you are asked to drain it, you can do it without passing out before dessert. You should make at least one toast, and if your hosts are important to you, make several to the success of a venture, friendship, and so on.

Bathroom Facilities

It is likely that just about the only time you will find a familiar style of bathroom in China will be in a first-class hotel room. Few public places (not even airports), private homes, or offices will be able to accommodate you in the manner to which you have become accustomed, although even this past truism is changing, as more sit-down toilets are being purchased by businesses and even private people.

If you are traveling within China, take some bathroom tissue with you. Most places will have paper now, but some will not. Don't be unpleasantly surprised. You will also most likely be unhappy with the cleanliness of restroom facilities, so take whatever you might need (a toilet seat cover, toilet tissue, an antiseptic wipe or spray, etc.).

Proper Dress

Dress formally unless told otherwise, especially for formal meetings outside the workplace. It's a sign of respect and sincerity. In the work environment, if your counterparts wear work clothes, it's okay for you to dress somewhat informally.

Don't wear bright colors. Red is the color of celebration in China. Be careful of white, which is their "death" color. Don't wear white shoes or socks.

Personal Behavior

When speaking, the Chinese stand closer to each other than we do, so try not to back away.

To act too informally shows disrespect, so don't loosen your tie, or put your feet up.

Our facial expressions tend to show our emotions. Try to control that tendency. Americans' expressions tend to give away such negotiating emotions as frustration, upset, and anger. The Chinese consider any such show of emotions childish. Talk slowly and deliberately, and try not to use idioms or slang, which are easily misunderstood by interpreters.

Try not to interrupt your counterparts when they are speaking, but be prepared for them to interrupt any conversation between you and your associates. They are not being impolite; it just that while Americans are used to hearing many languages other than our own, the Chinese are not. If you are speaking English, it's as though you are humming, and it's okay to interrupt humming.

Try not to act as though you are in a hurry. If you have another appointment, give early warning of it, so you can break off easily without seeming impolite by trying to leave on short notice.

Don't leave your belongings lying around in business centers, offices, and so on. If you leave a possession somewhere with the intention of picking it up later, be sure that you won't have problems. The Chinese have a habit of locking things up without giving you access to where your possessions are.

Business Cards

Business cards should be double-sided (Chinese on one side and English on the other). You will need a Chinese printer to do this. Ask a Chinese associate to help. You can get Chinese-language cards done very quickly and cheaply in China, but remember that the printers very likely don't know English.

Pay attention to the translation of a logo, business name, or motto. Make sure someone who is fluent in Chinese translates for you before printing. There are often different options for translation. If your name or motto doesn't translate well, or it has a negative connotation in Chinese, create substitute Chinese words or choose an alternative translation with better connotations.

Read business cards that you are given immediately. To not do so shows a lack of interest or disrespect. Offer and receive business cards with both hands. It's also a sign of respect.

The Chinese Calendar and Holidays

The Chinese calendar is different from the Gregorian (or Western) calendar, which begins each year on January 1 and ends on December 31. The Chinese calendar is based upon lunar cycles. As a result, it starts on a different Gregorian date each year, between January 21 and February 19. The lunar calendar repeats over twelve years; hence, the Chinese astrology chart based upon the year born, and having twelve different major classifications. See Appendix 5 (Chinese Holidays) and Appendix 6 (The Chinese Zodiac).

Be sure to have an accurate chart of holidays for the period during which you will be traveling. The Chinese take their holidays seriously. It is family time. Workers travel back to their home city, and business owners devote this time to their families. Therefore, three-day holidays are longer than three days to allow travel to and from the family city. Trying to conduct business at this time is like trying to do business in America between Christmas and New Year's.

Corruption and Gift-Giving

What you may call corruption is widespread in China. Although the government launched a high-profile anti-corruption campaign, these efforts are hampered by the lack of truly independent investigative bodies.

Corruption does not involve only foreigners, by any means. The system of official corruption was in place long before foreign companies were allowed to do business in China.

One recent case concerned official corruption in the domestic coal mining industry, which supplies more than 70 percent of China's energy needs. The industry has been plagued with a series of mining disasters. Last year close to 5,000 miners lost their lives in mining accidents. There had been many allegations of official corruption involving safety inspection approvals and accident cover-ups for pay.

The government finally sent independent investigators to probe the allegations. They identified more than 4,500 officials who were guilty of some form of illegal behavior involving money.

Gift-giving to gain favored treatment is a difficult subject. In China, there is a certain cultural acceptance of that practice, but always within cultural guideline limits. Cases are brought to the fore when they exceed those limits. In some instances, giving gifts is an alternative to strict interpretation and enforcement of regulations and taxes, as well as speeding up the acceptance of applications and proposals. (For more on this, read the section on the Foreign Corrupt Practices Act [FCPA] in Chapter 6.)

Your dilemma comes in knowing that most Chinese purchasing agents have been favored by your competitors, which does influence their decisions. If you are to establish the kind of personal relationship that is necessary to receive orders from those purchasing agents, some favors probably will be involved.

I am not advocating that you practice corruption or significant gift-giving, but you need to be aware of its existence and its basis in the culture. It does not carry the same stigma that it carries here. Most trouble comes when you do not make gift-giving a private affair or when it exceeds the limits of propriety.

If the gift-giving is in the form of money, and is quasi official, such as the quid pro quo that the government will do certain things if money is paid, promised performance has been known to lag once money is paid. Also, government officials change, and the promises of the last official may not be honored by the present one. For that matter, the promises may not be honored by the people who made them.

A case in point was an American company that was building a major factory. To do that, it acquired land from the government on which there were makeshift houses accommodating some people. The company agreed to pay the equivalent of $250,000 additional money to the government for relocation expenses for the dwellers. When the construction came close to the point at which it could not continue until all the land was cleared, there were still some squatters occupying the land. The company went to the government for help in moving the remaining people per the agreement. They were told that an additional $250,000 would be required. Even then, construction was delayed for some time.

On the other hand, there are some great success stories about companies doing favors to help the government achieve an important objective and then being rewarded with invaluable favors that the government granted in return. In dealing with government promises, the only thing certain is uncertainty.

The granting of favors and the returning of favors is a complex issue in China. One rule of thumb that might help is that favors you grant may not be repaid as you would like, if there is not a continuing reason why it would be in the Chinese recipient's best interest to return the favor.

One of our clients did a favor for a potential Chinese customer by obtaining some hard-to-get materials from a mutual supplier on an expedited schedule for the prospect. The American company carried considerable weight with the American supplier of the desired material, whereas the Chinese company did not. Our client was soon rewarded by a major first-time contract for its Chinese subsidiary from that prospect, who undoubtedly considered the fact that the intervention of the American company might be needed again in the future.

Sports, Entertainment, and Humor

Chinese like going to sports, public performances, and travel spots as family activities.

Popular sports in China include badminton, basketball, soccer, volleyball, table tennis, bowling, swimming, and gymnastics. So, if someone you are visiting has a teenage son, a Shaquille O'Neal or (of course) a Yao Ming official T-shirt will be greatly appreciated. Urban people are surprisingly knowledgeable about American sports, especially basketball.

Table tennis and badminton, neither of which is very popular in the United States, are national sports in China. If you play either of these very well, you'll have an easy time making friends. One businessman who had played in world table tennis tournaments reported that it has broken the ice for him many times and that the Chinese accord him greater respect, because they believe that no American can compete with the Chinese in this Chinese-dominated sport.

Most Chinese people appreciate a joke and have what you might call a good sense of humor. Americans have been able to establish good rapport quickly with an appropriate joke. Don't tell off-color jokes, or jokes that are language dependent, such as double-entendre jokes. Also, make sure that your interpreter understands and appreciates the joke before he tries to interpret it. As mentioned previously, some attempts at humor turn into disasters because of poor translation.

Even though the Chinese may appreciate your jokes, don't expect them to return the favor. They have few jokes, and are often reluctant to tell them.

Superstitions, the Zodiac, and Feng Shui

The Chinese have several popular superstitions. First, they have a strong belief in fortunetellers. Many will plan their lives around what their fortuneteller tells them.

Superstitions extend to colors; as mentioned earlier, red is a celebration color and white is a color of death. Chinese people won't have any animal that has white fur below the knee.

In numbers, four is unlucky. When you get a phone or cell phone, avoid the number four. Eight is a lucky number, and nine signifies long life. You will see many eights and nines in numbers there, such as telephone numbers for hotels or companies seeking prestigious numbers. In general, Chinese prefer even numbers to odd numbers.

They also believe in the accuracy of their animal zodiac signs, similar to our astrology horoscopes. They will marry, plan their families, and even choose partners according to the compatibility of their animal signs. For the years of the signs of the Chinese Zodiac, see Appendix 6.

You have probably heard of feng shui. The Chinese believe that feng shui should determine the location of buildings, doors, windows, and even furnishings. If you are opening a business there, you need to pay attention to feng shui, because everyone that you deal with will.

Religion

When the Communists first came to power, they rid the country of foreign missionaries and organized official state churches.

The government officially recognizes only five religions: Protestantism, Catholicism, Buddhism, Islam, and Taoism.

In the 1990s, in response to government loosening of strict control over the details of individual lives, there was a rapid rise in religion, especially in rural areas. It has now caught hold in cities, where it is enjoying rapid growth. Foreign researchers now estimate that there are about 50 million Protestants and Catholics in China. This may seem to be a small number in a country of 1.3 billion, but it compares to about only 6 million in 1980. The Christian religions have been actively trying to expand in China and have made significant progress.

The government still believes that the growth of religion may present a serious threat to the continuance of Communist rule and must be controlled. They believe that the spread of religion lessens their influence over people who practice their chosen faith and thus have another master.

Government regulations limit the distribution of Bibles, prevent proselytizing, and set forth strict rules on displaying religious symbols.

On the other hand, the government feels it should show tolerance and accommodate the rise of religion, including Christianity, to appease foreign countries and people who are providing substantial and growing foreign investment in China and to prevent domestic unrest. Today China uses its official state churches to supervise congregations and monitor religious followers. There are also some "underground" churches that operate in secret.

It is surprising that no major religion has originated in China. The country is now officially atheist, but in fact, many Chinese take a practical point of view and worship at a Buddhist temple if they are visiting an area where one is a point of interest. The most important religions are still Buddhism and Taoism, followed by Islam and Christianity. Islam is widely practiced only in western China. Xinjiang Uygur West region is almost 50 percent Islamic.

Religion is not a major part of the lives of the great majority of Chinese people, although with the easing of governmental control over their daily lives, more people are visiting religious shrines at least once in a while.

Many people passively accept Buddhism. They may pray to Buddha and ask him for favors, but they do not actively worship regularly.

Most Chinese people, even those who are nonreligious, believe in an afterlife. They honor their dead and say prayers and have conversations with them at the gravesite. They bring gifts for them including special paper symbolizing money, and paper mockups of useful types of conveniences. These paper items are burned at the site, signifying that they are to go to heaven, where the deceased is residing.

As noted previously, white is worn as the mourning color, not black.

Smoking

The majority of Chinese do smoke. If you're a smoker, you'll like this aspect, but if not, this is a potential problem area. Be prepared for some secondhand smoke. Some places, such as elevators, display "no smoking" signs. You should honor them, but some Chinese will not.

If you are at a restaurant and sitting near smokers, try coughing. They will ask if the smoke bothers you, and you can reluctantly say that you don't smoke and sometimes it affects you. They usually will courteously refrain, or at least direct the smoke away from you. Don't directly ask them to stop smoking. Smoking has not been outlawed at restaurants and bars, and in fact is prevalent in those places.

Weather

You can't ask what the weather is like in China any more than you can ask what the weather is like in America. It depends on the city and the time of the year. As you might expect, northern China is cold and southern China is warmer, but northern China seems to be colder than the northern United States by a good bit, as it gets the winds coming down from Siberia.

An American from New England thought that he knew cold and took a walk around the block early one winter morning in Changchun in Jilin Province, north of Beijing. He said that he thought he would lose parts of both ears and the tip of his nose. As the Boy Scouts say, "Be prepared." Appendix 8 lists the average temperatures in January and July for key cities, along with average precipitation. That should give you some idea of what to expect. If the city you'll be visiting is not one of the ones listed, find it on a map and look for the closest one listed in the appendix.

Tipping and Personal Gifts

Tipping is a Western custom. The practice in China is rare and different. Don't tip cabdrivers or most restaurant servers. Hotel personnel are among the few who are accustomed to tips, but much lower ones than in the United States. Figure that there are 12 cents per yuan. For a bellman, 1 yuan per large suitcase is considered a good tip. When in doubt, the rule of thumb is: Don't tip unless you feel that you received very special service.

Regarding personal gifts, you should understand that, socially speaking, the Chinese are very generous people. Protocol and appearances are very important. Don't try to compliment anything that your hosts are wearing or portable personal items that they own. It is customary for them to give the items to you, and they will insist that you take them.

Before we began briefing our clients on "dos" and "don'ts," one American made the mistake of complimenting a Chinese business acquaintance on his company jacket. Immediately, the acquaintance whipped off the jacket and handed it to the surprised American, complete with packs of cigarettes in the pockets, and insisted that he accept it.

As a sign of respect, offer and accept gifts with both hands. Do not be insulted if a Chinese person does not open your gift in your presence. Many will open gifts only when they are alone.

Dangerous Assumptions

Here is an area that is certainly affected by the other three problem areas—language, culture, and customs—but in a way, it's more insidious because you don't suspect a problem. It's that part of communications where you *think* that you understand each other, but you're each making completely different assumptions about the same things.

In a typical case, two sides will be approaching discussions from different perspectives and with different assumptions. The manner in which you do things and your normal practices and experiences lead you to make assumptions about the other side's thinking that are not true.

Does "profit" mean the same thing to you that it means to the other side? Does "risk"? Do you both have the same accounting standards, procedures, methods, and practices?

The answer is no, and you need to be acutely aware of areas of possible future conflict.

Some of the most bothersome areas are those that are culturally based and not easily identified as even a potential issue.

One of these is the way the Chinese view agreements. They can make (or say that they made) an assumption about areas of a contract that you take for granted. You assume that if an area is not discussed, it does not apply. For example, if special tooling was not discussed, you may assume that it is included in the price and will be surprised when you receive a bill for it. The same applies to sample costs, special services costs, or any other costs normally included in prices in the United States. (See Chapter 13 for more about negotiating and making agreements.)

Chapter 6

Money, Banking, and Legal Issues

CHINA'S BANKING SYSTEM has undergone significant changes in the last two decades. The country has been trying to transform its banking industry into viable Western-style financial institutions and has contributed more than $60 billion to that effort. The result is that banks are now functioning much more like banks in the West than ever before. Nevertheless, China's banking industry has remained in the government's hands even though banks have gained more autonomy. China's accession to WTO promises to lead to a significant opening of this industry to foreign participation.

China may limit foreign bank expansion to less developed areas (western China) to protect local banks from competition before bank law liberalization this year (2006).

Foreign banks cannot sell their own credit cards until the end of 2006, when the ban against their offering credit to Chinese individuals will be lifted. It is reasonably certain that foreign financial institutions and Chinese banks will join forces, because the foreign firms need the network of offices and contacts that the Chinese banks have and the Chinese banks need the international banking experiences and the credit card and consumer credit experience that the foreign companies have.

In banking, insurance, and some other industries in which China faces a rush of international competition from superpower foreign companies that are already experienced, entrenched, powerful, and have high-level contacts, Chinese counterparts need the experience and foreign training necessary to combat such formidable foes.

If they plan to raise capital and list securities abroad, Chinese businesses certainly need the experience and knowledge base to do it. Consequently, many Chinese banks are forming partnerships and liaisons with international banking powerhouses. Other banks are trying to recruit experienced, high-level executives from the internationals.

The Banking System

At the top of the system is China's central bank, the People's Bank of China (PBOC), which has been charged with managing the money supply and credit and supervising the banking system. PBOC, together with SAFE (State Administration of Foreign Exchange), sets foreign-exchange policies.

The PBOC supervises the banking sector's payment, clearing, and settlement systems, and audits the operations and balance sheets of all financial institutions in China. In addition, it implements the regulations regarding the operation of the commercial banks.

Commercial Banks

In 1995, the government introduced the Commercial Bank Law to commercialize the operations of the four state-owned banks:

- The Bank of China (BOC) specializes in foreign-exchange transactions and trade finance. It is estimated that BOC holds a 59 percent share of China's trade-finance business.
- The China Construction Bank (CCB) provides financing to infrastructure projects and urban housing development.
- The Agriculture Bank of China (ABC) specializes in providing financing to China's agricultural sector and

offers wholesale and retail banking services to farmers, township and village enterprises (TVEs), and other rural institutions.

- The Industrial and Commerce Bank of China (ICBC), now the largest bank in China, is the major supplier of funds to China's urban areas and manufacturing sector.

Second-Tier Commercial Banks

In addition to the big four state-owned commercial banks, there are smaller commercial banks. The largest ones in this group include the Bank of Communication, China Everbright Bank, CITIC Industrial Bank, Shanghai Pudong Development Bank, Shenzhen Development Bank, Guangdong Development Bank, Minsheng Bank, and Hua Xia Bank. The second-tier banks are generally healthier in terms of asset quality and profitability and have much lower non-performing loan ratios than do the big four.

PBOC has encouraged banks to diversify their portfolios by increasing their services to the private sector and individuals. In July 2000, a personal credit rating system was launched in Shanghai to be used to assess consumer credit risk and set ratings standards. This is an important move in developing China's consumer credit industry, and for increasing bank loans to individuals.

The central government has allowed several small banks to raise capital through bonds or stock issues, which has set a precedent.

The Availability of General Financing

In China's liberalized economic regime, there are many ways to finance imports. The most commonplace are letters of credit and documentary collections. Under these methods, foreign exchange is allocated by the central government for an approved import.

One source of financial support available to U.S.-based exporters is the Export-Import Bank of the United States

(Ex-Im Bank). This independent agency of the U.S. government exists to increase the competitive position of U.S.-based exporters in overseas markets by assisting in the financing of U.S. export sales.

Ex-Im Bank guarantees the repayment of loans or makes loans to international purchasers of U.S. goods and services. Ex-Im Bank also extends export credit insurance to overseas buyers and protects U.S. exporters from the risks of non-payment for political or commercial reasons. There must be a reasonable assurance of repayment on every transaction financed.

Ex-Im Bank has signed master credit agreements with Bank of China and China Development Bank, but it can work with any Chinese bank that meets its credit guidelines.

For more information concerning Ex-Im Bank programs and application procedures contact Ex-Im Bank in Washington, D.C., at (800) 565-EXIM (3946) or (202) 565-3946. In China, contact the Ex-Im Bank Chief Officer (at this writing, Craig Allen), at the Foreign Commercial Service, U.S. Embassy, Beijing, Tel: (86-10) 8529-6655, x801; Fax: (86-10) 8529-6558. Exposure fee calculations and applications can be found online at *www.exim.gov.*

Regarding China's conversion and transfer (foreign exchange) policies, all foreign-invested enterprises (FIEs) in China are entitled to open and maintain foreign exchange accounts for current account and capital account transactions. In order to do so, an FIE must first apply to SAFE for permission; for going concerns, permission is usually quick and easy.

Large state-owned enterprises (SOEs) continue to receive the bulk of commercial bank lending, but this is rapidly changing, and local financing of FIEs is becoming more widely available. Again, friendships and good relations are extremely important.

Foreign firms that need working capital, whether foreign exchange or local currency, may obtain short-term loans from China's state-owned commercial banks. However, priority lending is often given to investments that bring in advanced technology or produce goods for export.

Since 1998, Chinese interest rates have generally been lower than those in other parts of the world, making it more attractive to explore onshore financing. Some FIEs have used local financing in China to keep the debt off their U.S. balance sheets.

China has now put into effect a "security law," the first national legislation covering mortgages, liens, pledges, and guaranties. The law defines debtor and guarantor rights and provides for mortgaging of property, including land and buildings, as well as other tangible assets such as machinery, aircraft, and other types of vehicles.

While some areas of the law remain unclear, such as how the transfer of property under foreclosure is affected, the law represents an important step forward. Chinese commercial banks have successfully repossessed vehicles from delinquent borrowers. Banks may welcome foreign investors to take over non-performing loans and the underlying collateral, but more enabling regulations need to be enacted.

Private firms still have serious difficulties in raising capital. However, even this is changing. With the tremendous growth in the private sector, larger private enterprises have successfully borrowed money against assets.

There also is a huge growth in money loaned for property purchase and private construction as a result of the new private property legislation. The percentage of money loaned against real estate and construction will increase with the establishment and growth of a viable real estate market for privately owned real property.

Some foreign-owned companies have been successful, after proper introductions, in negotiating loans with commercial banks. First, a personal relationship has to be established and nurtured by the principals; then, with the sharing of financial information on an ongoing basis, along with anecdotal information about the company's exploits, loans on assets such as equipment and receivables can be forthcoming.

Although most banks and personnel are unsophisticated in the creative financing area, once you break through the formal exterior they are willing and almost anxious to learn, especially if you relate details of loans you have or have had with American banks.

It also helps if you have obtained any kind of loan on your China operations from your American bank. The Chinese are then motivated to compete. They feel that they should ultimately provide the business financing necessary for China's business, even with foreign companies.

Legal and Accounting Concerns

If you intend to draft a formal, legally enforceable agreement, you must cover every point of possible conflict. Any agreement should be written by an attorney familiar with the requirements of Chinese business law. It must be written both in Chinese and in English.

There is a problem in choosing an attorney. Foreign lawyers are not permitted to qualify to practice law in China and are not allowed to form a joint venture with Chinese lawyers. If you choose an American, he cannot represent you in court and will not have court experience there. If you choose a Chinese attorney, he may not fully understand your goals and concerns. In choosing a Chinese attorney, spend some time interviewing him to be sure that you communicate well.

You have already heard several times about the importance of accurate translation. With a formal legal agreement, accurate and exact translation of meaning is absolutely vital. Even if you have no intention of bringing suit in China, detailed agreements prevent misunderstandings later.

China has had consistent dynamic economic growth, which has led to continuous rapid transformations in the domestic economy. Nothing is fixed. Thus, when entering into a contract with a Chinese partner you must be careful to plan for all foreseeable contingencies. Make sure that your attorney keeps up-to-date not only on what has recently changed, but also on what is about to change.

Furthermore, no matter how nonlitigious you may be, you may be faced with initiating a lawsuit or defending a suit here in America.

The Chinese Legal System

Chinese society is in transition from rule by man to rule by law. Most laws are general; details are specified in implementing regulations.

Laws and regulations in China tend to be far more general than in most Organization for Economic Cooperation and Development (OECD) countries. This vagueness allows Chinese courts and officials to apply them flexibly, which results in ruling and judgment inconsistencies.

Having to accommodate opposite needs makes for an ambivalent attitude, which translates into ambiguous rules and uneven application of those rules and a lack of transparency and predictability. This problem permeates China; lack of specificity in laws, rules, and regulations means that people, foreign and domestic, don't know if and when their actions will be sanctioned. This makes for a lack of bold action and much time spent on making friends who can vouch for you if you overstep the invisible line.

While there seems to be no shortage of rules and regulations, there are few procedures in place to appeal regulatory decisions.

U.S. Foreign Corrupt Practices Act (FCPA)

The Foreign Corrupt Practices Act was passed in 1977 and revised in 1988. The provisions of the FCPA prohibit the bribery of foreign government officials by U.S. persons and companies and set out accounting and record-keeping rules.

The anti-bribery provisions of the FCPA apply to any U.S. person, and they make it illegal for U.S. persons to bribe a foreign government official for the purpose of obtaining or retaining business.

The FCPA deals only with bribes made to foreign government officials and does not cover payments to foreign persons who are not government officials. Furthermore, FCPA addresses only bribes that are intended for the purpose of obtaining or retaining business and does not address payments made to expedite or secure the performance of normal government actions, such as obtaining permits or licenses, processing official papers, clearing goods through Customs, loading and unloading cargo, and providing police protection.

For the full text of the FCPA, go to *www.usdoj.gov/criminal/fraud/fcpa/fcpastat.htm*.

Other American laws prohibit transfer of some sensitive technologies without a license. For more information on BIS (Bureau of Industry and Security) regulations, check *www.bis.doc.gov*.

Accounting Practices

Chinese law requires representative offices and FIEs to engage the services of accountants registered in China to prepare the official submissions of annual financial statements and other specified financial documents. Therefore, only Chinese accountants and joint venture accounting firms may provide these services.

All the Big Four accounting firms (KPMG International; Price Waterhouse Coopers; Deloitte Touche Tohmatsu; and Ernst and Young) have established offices in China and provide services ranging from providing advice on taxation matters and preparation of investment feasibility studies to setting up accounting systems that are in compliance with Chinese law.

It is very difficult to find an accounting firm that gₗ
you anything more than historical perspective. Chinese
accounting firms may be used to fulfill government reporting requirements, but you will need your own American-
trained accountants for top-level accounting input to help
make managerial decisions.

It is customary in China to have multiple sets of books
with different figures for different purposes. Most companies
have more than one and some have as many as five—one set
for the government supervising authorities, one set for tax
reporting, one set for the public, one set for investors, and
one set for internal use.

Intellectual Property Rights

The traditional Chinese view of intellectual property (IP) is
very different from ours. The Chinese people give lip service
to intellectual property, but traditionally, most of them really
believe that IP belongs to society, not individuals. Not even
people in charge of enforcement seem to understand and
support IP rights. Therefore, knocking off someone else's
product is a question of "Can I get away with it?" rather than
"Is it ethical or legal?"

The fundamental problems with enforcing IP rights rules
go beyond the fact that the Chinese people do not believe
philosophically in the basic rights of intellectual property,
however. What's even more important, in the new atmo-
sphere of Chinese pragmatism, is that enforcement is not
in China's economic interest. As is stated in the section that
follows, China makes money on counterfeiting, not on protecting the rights of foreigners.

Beijing's protestations that it is making every effort to
protect IP rights sound hollow when certain facts come
to light. It would seem that the perfect items to counterfeit in China would be 2008 Beijing Games logo products,
but searching for these items is futile. A search through the
Silk Street market in Beijing, which is one of the largest

ketplaces in the country, turns up a pleth-
it branded products of all kinds, but no fake

ed a law in 2002 specifically protecting the
intellectual property rights of its Olympic symbols. The
penalties for selling fake Olympic products carries far greater
penalties than those for other counterfeits. The 2004 Olympics brought Athens almost $900 million from the rights and
licenses of its logo. China is expecting its logo payoff to be
in excess of $1 billion, and it is the main source of funds for
the Games.

Naturally, foreign firms losing vast sums of money to
counterfeiters in China wonder why China isn't more effective in protecting the logos of foreign firms.

There is some evidence that the government is starting
to change its attitude toward unbridled misuse of intellectual
property, as it starts to realize that if it is to prosper in the
international market in the long term, its domestic industry
must develop its own technology and brand. Look for much
lip service and few results until China is convinced that IP
protection is in its best interest.

Another factor is that as yet the Chinese have not developed enough intellectual property for there to be a complete
understanding of how intellectual property rights protect
people and encourage them to create. There also is not complete understanding of the importance of the basic creative
process to the economy, to the creators, and to the quality
and enjoyment of life.

China also takes some liberties with patent protection
if it may severely affect royalties owed by Chinese, such as
the current third-generation technical standards issues now
being played out.

Counterfeiting and Pirating

Similar to the Chinese attitude toward intellectual
property is the country's attitude toward counterfeiting. If

patents and copyrights are not respected, then why should trademarks, logos, and other creative works such as movies or books be any different? The answer is that they aren't.

The music industry will tell you of $200 million in U.S. music being sold to China, and many times that amount in sales lost from pirating. The not-so-funny joke is that China owns one paid copy of everything.

Many of the Chinese will counterfeit anything that they can make money on. There is lax enforcement of international IP laws. If neither government officials nor those charged with day-to-day enforcement of IP laws believe in them, you can't expect these laws to be honored.

The Business Software Alliance (BSA), a U.S. trade group, estimates that 92 percent of the software used in China is counterfeit. That makes China the worst offender of piracy laws. In the United States, 22 percent of software is counterfeit, the BSA says. Those figures show that there is a big difference in attitude between the two countries, though the United States will still need to clean up its own house in order to authoritatively address the Chinese situation.

Counterfeiting in general is now estimated at $25 billion, or 8 percent of China's GDP. Counterfeiting seems concentrated in Fujian and Guangdong provinces. Fujian is the province nearest Taiwan and is influenced by Taiwan; Guangdong, the Chinese capital for electronics goods, is the province nearest Hong Kong and under its influence.

In my opinion, it is imperative that our own government give higher priority to stopping the counterfeiting business in China. It threatens the very existence of creative work in the world, and the United States is the world's creative capital. If there is little potential profit to be had from creative endeavors, why risk spending the time and effort creating anything? China needs to be convinced that the crime of counterfeiting is on a par with stealing tangible private property. However, because China benefits tremendously from this activity and there is no significant downside, there is little hope of stricter enforcement until the government sees the advantages on its own and changes its emphasis—or until other governments take a firmer stance.

The gist of the IP and counterfeiting problem is that China has not been susceptible to jawboning, cajoling, or empty threats. Promises without specifics, agreements without deadlines, and regulations without enforcement are just window dressing. All appeals for fairness, equity, justice, and goodwill are meaningless to Beijing. This problem will not be solved until Beijing is made to realize that it is in China's best economic interest to take meaningful action.

Protecting Your Intellectual Property

The question then is how to protect yourself from having your intellectual property knocked off. Having a legal confidentiality agreement is a requirement that attempts to deter this activity, but to protect yourself from harm in a practical manner requires ingenuity.

In manufacturing, the best protection is to leave out key ingredients, subassemblies, or processes that a manufacturer needs to complete the product that it is making—something that can be added after manufacture. There are proprietary products that are wholly produced in China, but by two or three different manufacturers, and then assembled in the United States. Before incurring major expense to protect your proprietary products and ideas, give some thought to practical, creative, simple, disguised, and surreptitious concepts that will do the job.

At a minimum, it is advisable to register copyrights and/or patents in China, but in the quest for practical protection, use the pragmatic protection approach described. Don't give anyone a chance to steal your proprietary property.

Legal enforcement in these cases is unpredictable. Sometimes you will be vindicated, but sometimes not. Don't depend on it.

Copyright and Patent Laws

As part of its protocols of accession to the WTO, China has committed to full compliance with the Agreement on Trade-Related Aspects of Intellectual Property (TRIP), as well as other TRIP-related commitments. During 2000 and 2001, China completed a revised patent law. China has also revised its trademark and copyright laws to ensure consistency with TRIP requirements.

So China does have copyright and patent laws. The problem is that violators are rarely prosecuted, says Jesse Feder, a director at the trade group BSA. That makes it easy for Chinese companies to copy designs from foreign competitors. Also, there's still a corruption factor in China.

On the other hand, China does see trade-secret protection as in its best interests. Trade-secret protection is widely pursued by Chinese and foreign companies in China, with a relatively large volume of trade-secret litigation being handled by Chinese courts.

China's Law to Counter Unfair Competition (1993) defines unfair competition to include conduct that infringes the "lawful rights" of another business, including acts that violate "commercial secrets" rights. Commercial secrets are defined as information that can bring economic benefits to the authorized users and that can be protected by taking appropriate security measures, including not making technical and operational information available to the public.

The Patent Process

For readers who may be involved with patents, or just for future information, this section summarizes the key points of the patent process as it is today. Remember, though, that the laws and the enforcement of them change according to the current thinking of the government, and that thinking is now tilting toward stricter enforcement.

China is coming to realize that it must come to grips with the intellectual property rights (IPR) issue. There are already laws on the books, but enforcement has varied from lax to nonexistent. Chinese patent law was legislated in 1984 and revised in 1992 and again in 2000.

Current legislation defines three types of patents: invention patents, utility model patents, and industrial design patents.

Applications and other documents relating to patents need to be submitted to the State Intellectual Property Office (SIPO).

The regulations set forth certain requirements for processing principles, and conform to the Patent Cooperation Treaty (PCT). Principles are spelled out for Chinese inventions, first-to-file principles, and the examination process itself, among other details.

Invention documents must include a detailed description of the request, specifications including claims and descriptions, pictures and drawings (if applicable), and an abstract summarizing the points of the document.

Any amendments after the application cannot address any points beyond the specifications and images included in the original application. Upon receiving an application, the SIPO records the filing date, issues a filing number, and notifies the applicant. The SIPO categorizes applications using the International Patent Classification (IPC). There is a preliminary check of applications to assure that they conform to the patent law and its regulations.

The classifications department of SIPO categorizes the application's subject matter and issues complete classification symbols for the inventive contents and an indexing code of these symbols if necessary.

Other documents related to the application, whether submitted at the same time or later, also are checked for conformity to the Patent Law and its regulations. Such additional documents are also checked for timeliness and for appropriate payments and timing of payments.

Applicants are given the opportunity to correct errors in an application or at least to identify them. Applications are rejected only after the applicant cannot remove or correct the error.

If the SIPO finds in its preliminary investigation that the application meets its requirements, the application will be published eighteen months after the filing date, or earlier, if the applicant so requests.

The applicant has three years from the filing date to request a substantive examination to determine whether patent rights will be granted. The application must meet all the requirements of the Patent Law, including those of "novelty, inventiveness, and practical applicability." The SIPO can, at its own option, conduct a substantive examination without a request. If the applicant does not request a substantive examination within the time limit, the application will be withdrawn.

It is important that the applicant keep in touch with the SIPO for status updates and thoroughly understand any problems, including type, form, and content of the response that is necessary; time limits; and fees. Many patent applications have been rejected because of poor communication.

In the search for documents similar to the application, the SIPO uses published descriptions of Chinese invention patent applications, Chinese patents for utility models, European patent applications, PCT international patent applications, and U.S. patent specifications.

The specified time limit for answering the first Office Action (a formal query questioning aspects of the patent) is usually four months. If required, other Office Actions are issued.

Usually, Office Actions are answered in writing within the time limit, but you may request an interview in person or attempt to satisfy minor objections by phone.

Chapter 7

Traveling in China

WHEN TRAVELING IN CHINA, a trip (logistics) coordinator needs to be designated. The coordinator should be in charge of the detailed arrangements of the trip: the passports, visas, travel and hotel reservations, keeping the appointment schedule, and the necessary material and equipment purchase or provision. The coordinator should also be in charge of intra-China travel, money exchange, restaurant arrangements, and all other details of the trip.

Obviously, the coordinator is very important to the success of your mission. Ideally, your translator should serve as your coordinator. It is a great advantage to speak the language when negotiating prices and making arrangements, but he must also be very knowledgeable and current about China today.

The coordinator could also act as cultural adviser and conduct lessons in culture, language, and behavior, but unless he is current and experienced in successfully dealing with the Chinese, you will still need an expert to help you source and negotiate.

If this project is important and crucial enough, and your budget is big enough, hire someone in-house for this position. His competence will weigh heavily on your odds of success.

The problem with recruiting the right person is the same as for any key person: it is very difficult to find the right blend of skills. This person has to speak two languages very fluently, and know the culture and customs of both. He also has to have a good head for business and keen perception in ferreting out the objectives and motivations of all of the parties.

If you do not have someone already and your budget does not allow for a permanent addition, consider hiring an expert from outside on a project basis. The right expert, with experience, will probably save you most of what you will pay him, just in negotiating cost savings for the accommodation arrangements he makes. The benefits he brings in terms of time savings, increased comfort level, avoidance of problems, professionalism, and increased odds of success on your trip should make this a worthwhile investment.

If your budget is more limited, you might consider hiring an expert on a time basis. This person is contacted by phone for specific projects or appointments. The major advantage of this service is that the cost is lower. You do whatever you can on your own and use the expert only on an as-needed and when-needed basis.

Hotel Accommodations

You will find the better hotels in China surprisingly good, comfortable, and inexpensive, with excellent service. It pays to discover which are the better ones in every city.

Rates are definitely open to negotiation. If you know someone in the city, or if you are visiting a large business in the city, you are more likely to get a preferred rate.

The beds are almost uniformly very hard. Some are so hard that it's like sleeping on the floor. If you know that a bed that hard will interfere with your sleep pattern, make the hardness of the bed a consideration for booking the hotel. Some five-star hotels don't have an alternative to the extra-hard bed. That is, no rooms have soft beds. If you are forced to book a hotel that only has extra-hard beds, and you are concerned about it, bring a thick pad with you. The hotel will also provide extra blankets for padding. Even so, you may have to get used to sleeping on hard beds.

When making your hotel reservations, you might want to make the TV one of your criteria. First find out which English-language channels they have. Most top hotels have at least CNN. Some four- and five-star hotels don't have even one English-language channel. That can get somewhat annoying if you want to keep abreast of the news or if you plan on spending much time in your room.

Business Centers and the Internet

Most good hotels in China have a business center with a fax machine and an Internet connection. Prices vary widely. Few hotels have anyone with more than a rudimentary understanding of English manning the business centers. If it's important that you get Internet access in a timely fashion, have someone you can call who speaks Chinese and can explain a particular problem, computer or otherwise, to the attendant. Lacking that, ask the attendant to call the best English speaker in the hotel.

Many post offices have Internet service or an Internet store nearby. Keep in mind that although prices for services outside the hotel are usually much lower, communicating your needs is more difficult.

If you are Internet dependent, you probably carry a laptop or notebook computer with you. Most of the better hotels now have Internet connections in at least some rooms. The cost is usually low, and the service may even be free. You might add this to the list of questions for your facilitator to ask. This cuts your dependence on the business center, cuts costs, and prevents you from being limited by the center's availability and hours.

Unfortunately, the pronouncement of availability is not always borne out in practice. Some hotels say that room access to the Internet is available, but for some reason, you can't get it. Remember that you need an electrical converter for your computer. Don't rely on the hotel's furnishing you one unless they guarantee it.

Travel Papers: Passports and Visas

To travel to China you will need a U.S. passport for each person making the trip. If you don't have a valid passport, get the application form at your local post office. Allow six weeks from the time you mail the requisite information to receiving your passport. (Expedited processing within two weeks is available at a higher fee.)

U.S. citizens traveling to China must also obtain a Chinese visa before embarking on the trip. A few different types of visas are issued to visitors, including the tourist visa (Type L), which allows the bearer one or two entries to stay up to one month each time.

Short-term business visas (Type F) are issued to travelers who are invited to visit for business or research purposes. A formal invitation from a Chinese host organization is required to obtain this type of visa.

Business travelers on short-term excursions for meeting or site-visit purposes generally apply for either the Type L or Type F visa. Consult the Chinese Embassy or Consulate General about obtaining the right type of visa, or apply through a travel agency or consultant.

Business firms seeking to bring in exhibits and items for display should consult with Customs authorities for regulation on the procedures and to obtain copies of appropriate forms.

Goods imported into China for display or demonstration at trade shows and exhibitions are exempt from Customs duty, provided that they are re-exported within three months.

Reasonable quantities of items for personal use by short-term visitors may be imported duty-free. Other items, such as cameras, televisions, stereo equipment, computers, and tape recorders, must be declared and may be assessed a duty depending upon the item's value.

Note that baggage limits for intra-China travel are much less than international limits, so unless you can offload or store baggage, you may be subject to excess baggage fees when traveling by air within China.

Expatriate managers who are assigned to work in China need to apply for employment visas. On their first trip into China on the Z visa (a Z visa is for an employed alien and his family), they are entitled to bring reasonable personal and household-use items duty-free, including the otherwise duty-charged items such as VCRs, PCs, and video cameras.

Chinese visas may be obtained at the Embassy of the People's Republic of China at any Chinese consulate listed:

Chinese Embassy in Washington, DC
2201 Wisconsin Avenue, N.W., Washington, DC 20007
Tel: (202) 338-6688, (202) 588-9760
Fax: (202) 588-9760

Chinese Consulate General in Chicago, IL
100 West Erie Street, Chicago, IL 60610
Tel: (312) 803-0095
Fax: (312) 803-0110

Chinese Consulate General in Houston, TX
3417 Montrose Boulevard, Houston, TX 77006
Tel: (713) 520-1462
Fax: (713) 521-3064

Chinese Consulate General in Los Angeles, CA
443 Shatto Place, Los Angeles, CA 90020
Tel: (213) 807-8088
Fax: (213) 807-8091

Chinese Consulate General in New York, NY
520 12th Avenue, New York, NY 10036
Tel: (212) 244-9392
Fax: (212) 465-1708

Chinese Consulate General in San Francisco, CA
1450 Laguna Street, San Francisco, CA 94115
Tel: (415) 674-2900
Fax: (415) 563-0494

If you are anywhere near a consulate, go in person. Be sure to call first and get the hours of operation, as the offices may not be open 9 to 5. Take your passport with you. It usually takes one week, but you can get your visa processed in two days if you pay an expediting fee. You may go back to pick up the visa personally, or have someone pick it up for you. Don't lose the receipt that the consulate gives you when you apply. You will need it for pickup.

China is now in the process of streamlining some of its procedures for entry-exit long-term residents there and for frequent travel abroad. China has recently announced the availability of "green cards" for permanent residents.

There are four different categories of people who can get this new green card. Many people who will be living in China for extended periods of time could fit into the second category, which includes foreign citizens who make a relatively large direct investment in China.

Foreigners who are not eligible or do not intend to get the "green card" can now apply for one to five years of residence permits and multi-entry visas. You may apply to the entry-exit administrative division of the Beijing Municipal Public Security Bureau in Beijing.

Some Helpful Travel Tips

You may travel at any time of the year, but if you're going to anyplace north of the Yangtze River during the coldest six months of the year, be prepared for subfreezing temperatures. South of the Yangtze, buildings are rarely heated, though many places in that area can get chilly, even in summer.

Your Flight

Your trip to China will take about fifteen hours of nonstop flying from the West Coast, depending on the airline and route. Coming back is shorter. If you can avoid it, try not to take flights that stop before they get to China. You'll have a tough enough time adjusting to time changes without unnecessary wasted time in foreign airports.

The Chinese airlines are better about going to and from China without intermediate stops, but expect that the food will be of very low quality, and that Chinese travelers will get better service than you. This is not because the attendants don't like you; it's because they feel insecure speaking English. Business class provides much more comfort than coach, at lower rates than American carriers charge.

With the recent problems that the airlines are having, some American carriers with flights to China have sought a solution that involves combining flights with Chinese or other carriers. This means that planes presently tend to be pretty full, and since many Chinese planes have less leg room to begin with, it makes for some pretty uncomfortable economy-class flights.

Another potential difficulty can occur if there are crowded accommodations, as some passengers traveling on Chinese planes report seatmates who don't meet modern hygienic standards and who cough openly, increasing your health risk. This type of problem will become apparent early in the trip and you might request a seat change of an attendant, even if it causes some inconvenience.

If you haven't formed the habit of sleeping when traveling, you'd better start now or you will have a couple of bad days after you arrive. Many travelers have a much easier time going to China than coming back. You should sleep more than half the trip going there. Then, with a little extra sleep on the first day of arrival, you'll be ready to go.

On the way back, you might have a little more difficulty, needing a couple of days to get back in the groove. Sleeping on the trip as well as the day afterward is the key to a smooth adjustment.

Also, caffeine and alcohol have a negative effect on your adjustment—alcohol, more so. To help you cope with the travel, eat light, nutritious food, and drink more water and fruit juice than usual, both before the trip and during it (if possible).

Buying Medical Supplies

Don't count on easily buying too many common medical supplies in China. Take your medications, headache remedies, allergy and cough medicines, and so on with you. On the other hand, it is easy to get many pharmaceuticals, and you don't need a prescription. Many American brands are sold at the larger pharmaceutical chain stores, but not all of them. If you find what you want, though, it's much cheaper there.

Electricity

Remember that Chinese voltage is 220 volts, and be sure your equipment is compatible. Adapters and prong converters may be necessary. Hotels are supposed to have adapters for you to use, but some hotels' adapters don't work. If you take your own, you're safer.

Entertainment and Information Media

To play a VHS tape, you need to have it converted to a PAL format, or take along your own VCR. The Chinese have already almost completely switched to DVDs and CDs, though, so you're much better off in those media. Also, it's easier to find equipment for the newer media.

If you are a newspaper junkie, you may have a problem during your stay in China. Foreign papers are available, but they are at least one day old and mostly two or more days behind, and the government controls the news from Chinese sources. As mentioned earlier, there is only one news agency in China (named Xinhua), and that is strictly controlled by the government. All Chinese news sources must adhere to Xinhua's news guidelines. Actually, Chinese news is reasonably accurate except when there is a political issue involved. (For more on this, see the Censorship section in Chapter 2.)

Transportation in China

The most common ways that people get around in Chinese cities (from most often used to least) are walking; bicycle; motor scooter or motorcycle; bus; taxi; and private car. Most cars are still owned by government agencies and companies and are driven by professional drivers. However, the number of cars owned and operated by individuals is growing rapidly, especially in the larger urban centers. In some of the largest international cities, the number of personal drivers is approaching the number of professional drivers. This phenomenon is very recent and points out the explosive growth of individual automobile purchases.

In 2004, a survey estimated that three out of every thousand Chinese middle-class families owned their own private car. That figure is now grossly understated.

Driving in the City

The mass of people still get to and from work or shopping by bus, nonmotorized transportation, or motorbikes and motor scooters. Another noticeable trend is the increase of motor scooters relative to bicycles.

Traffic is becoming overwhelming. Traffic is a factor that should affect where you stay relative to where you're going within a city. Traffic and hotel location could add an hour each way in some large cities. The government has acknowledged the traffic problem, and serious, drastic solutions are being discussed. One proposal is to impose fees for driving into some central cities. Another is a new tax on large cars.

Your best bet for traveling to a company is to ask to be picked up, especially if your destination is a distance from where you are staying. Almost every Chinese company has its own car or can borrow a car and will be glad to pick you up at your hotel and take you back.

Taxi rates are quite inexpensive by American standards. If you use a taxi, make sure that the driver knows where he is going. If there is any doubt, call the business and have someone give him instructions. Most drivers have cell phones, or you can let them use yours if you have one.

Not all taxi companies are the same. Some are better (more honest) than others. Ask your hotel for reputations in that city. If your hotel has its own cabs, they most likely will be very good but carry a sizable price premium. In any case, remember that taxi drivers are not expecting a tip.

Depending on where you are and where you are going, some locations can only be accessed on that day by odd- or even-numbered license plates. Make sure that your taxi can get to where you're going before you start out.

Don't undertake to drive anywhere yourself. Even many of the Chinese who have driven for any length of time in America won't risk driving in China again. To say that Chinese drivers are aggressive is a great understatement. Traffic rules and laws are obeyed only intermittently. Going through stoplights, making left turns or U-turns from the right lanes, or right turns from left lanes, are all common.

Pedestrians and bicycles do not have the right of way in China, but they act as though they do.

Fortunately, vehicles drive on the right as in the United States, so that you don't have to worry about stepping off the curb looking left and getting run down by traffic coming from the right, as you would in England.

China has adopted traffic signs and many rules from the United States. Names of streets usually have English letters along with Chinese letters.

Drivers admire other drivers who are more aggressive than they are. If you are riding with a professional driver, occupy yourself or look out the side window. Looking out the front window will make you a candidate for an early heart attack.

Intercity Travel

In intercity travel, you have several choices: plane, bus, train, or private car. If you know the distance to your destination, you'll know which are impractical.

If you are traveling by plane, you will be comforted to know that the Chinese airlines' safety record is good.

If you have been to China before but not recently, you'll be happy to know that you are no longer required to pay separate fees, such as the airport construction fee. Any remaining fees are now part of the ticket price.

Another point to remember is that it is much cheaper to buy plane tickets for intra-China travel as much in advance as possible, but you must be in the city that you are leaving from before you make the purchase. Discount travel agents will not hold tickets for your arrival.

In China, going by train, and in many cases by bus, is a real alternative to planes. First, planes might not have the schedule or frequency you need; also, you can arrange good sleeping accommodations on trains, and with a little more discomfort, you can sleep on a bus.

If you're traveling by train overnight, apply as early as possible for a soft bed. If you can't get one, apply for a reserved hard bed. If you don't reserve, you won't get much sleep.

Many of the industrial cities that you might be interested in are a two- to four-hour bus trip from the main city in the region. Traveling these relatively short distances, up to four hours by bus, can be a nice, pleasant trip. You see the Chinese countryside in seats that are not too bad. Seats are usually available and the times are more convenient than those of a train, and do not require reservations.

When choosing your mode of transportation, balance your most important factors—cost, time, and convenience.

You will need to know the distances between cities, and also will need a map to see where they are in relation to each other. Your trip coordinator should be assigned to fulfilling this task. See Appendix 7 for a map of China with the key cities, and Appendix 9 for a chart of air distances between cities.

Air distances can be misleading. From Shanghai to Ningbo is only 90 air miles. However, there is a bay that separates them, and the travel time has been three and one-half to four hours. A bridge that spans the bay and cuts the travel time in half was recently completed.

Most Americans traveling in China make the same mistake that foreigners traveling in our country make. They assume that San Francisco and Los Angeles are right next door to each other, or that they can drive from Los Angeles to New York in time for dinner. Distances in China are great. Know distances and traveling times before planning a trip.

If the trip is less than four hours, and you are traveling to a particular company, see if that company will send a car for you. Many will, and it is the most comfortable way to go. It may also tell you how eager the company is to do business with you. Most companies have spacious vans, and many of them are American.

Money Exchange

As mentioned in Chapter 2, China's currency is the yuan (pronounced "yuen," not "yu-ann") or RMB (for *Ren Ming Bi*, "people's money"). Currently the exchange rate is about 7.95 yuan to the dollar. This is for exchanging spending money, not for doing business.

If you have a business deal going, and if your partner is sophisticated and is not trying to make money on the exchange rate, you can figure that he gets a "special benefit" from the government on the exchange rate of yuan to the dollar. So normally, any money to be paid to a business, or quotes received, should be in yuan.

If you do pay in yuan, arrange an acknowledged exchange rate, taking into account the special benefit. Let your source know that you know about the special benefit. He may not be willing to quote you using the special benefit, because he may consider the benefit to be his profit, but your knowing about it may help in sharpening his price quotations.

If you are making personal purchases in China, buy in yuan. Don't ask merchants or retailers to take U.S. currency; they will charge you the worst exchange rates, because they are the least familiar with currency exchange.

There are no restrictions on the amount of money you are allowed to carry into the country in U.S. currency for personal use without declaring it. But if you plan on taking more than a few hundred dollars back home, then declare what you are taking in, because no money is allowed out without permission except what you took in.

When you arrive in China, have a small amount in yuan for transportation, airport tips, and transportation to your hotel at least. From that point on, a nearby bank or the hotel can exchange money for you.

At one time, an acquaintance at your destination may have been able to exchange money for you at better rates, but that's not possible now. Rates at your hotel will be better than airport rates, which are the worst. A nearby bank is usually the best source for currency exchange. Many hotels do not carry much exchange currency, so plan to have a bank exchange the amount you need to make larger purchases.

Most merchants are not usually accustomed to exchanging currency or giving good rates, but occasionally you will find some that will. If you're dealing with merchants or private parties, make sure that the currency bills you receive show evidence of use. China does have a counterfeiting problem.

All major hotels accept Visa and MasterCard, and most now accept American Express. The exchange rates are usually standard, so you can use credit cards to conserve cash.

If you will have a recurring need for business money in China, or a one-time need for a large sum of money, arrange to be introduced to a banker with whom you will be able to form a relationship. Have him open a dollar account for you in China. Send all information to your bank in the States to arrange to transfer money to China.

Chinese banks still don't have designated digits for which office the account is in, so you need a complete address for the bank in China, along with the digitized account number and Swift number, or the transfer will not be completed in a timely fashion. As part of the provisions of the Patriot Act, U.S. banks are now requiring a physical address for the payee as well.

Transfer a sum of money as a trial before your need for money becomes pressing, in order to enable you to work out any kinks ahead of time. Transfers used to be completed within three or four business days, but nowadays it sometimes takes up to two weeks. To expedite receipt, get the confirmation number of the transaction from your bank and forward that information to your bank in China.

Foreign-invested enterprises (FIEs) are permitted to keep foreign exchange in foreign-exchange accounts at commercial banks. China has required that FIEs submit an annual report on their foreign-currency transactions, known as the Foreign-Exchange Examination Report. Once the report is approved, firms receive a stamped Foreign Exchange Registration Certificate that enables them to obtain foreign exchange.

China now allows all FIEs in China to buy and sell foreign currency and exchange RMB in authorized banks for trade and services, debt payment, and profit repatriation. China's stated goal of achieving a fully convertible currency remains distant because of political concerns over the potential impact to the Chinese economy, and the authorities refuse to commit to a specific timetable for capital account liberalization.

Communications and Cell Phones

The best way to keep in touch both with people back home and your contacts in China is to buy your own cell phone when you get there and get a number assigned to you.

When you buy your cell phone, also buy cell calling cards for domestic and foreign use. If you get the plan with no minimum monthly charge, you pay more per minute, but it will be much cheaper in the long run if you are not in the country more than half the time. You can then use that phone and number each time you go. Having your own cell phone is more convenient and is cheaper than any alternative, unless you have a landline you can use at your convenience.

It is much cheaper to call from the United States to China than from China to the United States, so instruct people in the United States on exactly how to dial to reach you. To call China from America, first dial 011 to designate an international call, then dial 86, the country code for China, followed by the region or city code, and then the number. If I were calling Shanghai, China, which has a city code of 21, for example, I might dial 011-86-21-5559-9999.

Although in America the area code and number are always ten digits, in China it may vary. For example, all cell phones, wherever purchased, have a three-digit code, always starting with "1." You are charged more if your phone is out of the purchase area when you make or receive calls, so buy your phone in the area where you plan to spend the most time.

Calling from your hotel is the most expensive way to make an international call. The cheaper way to go if you are initiating the call is to buy an international calling card that can be used from landlines.

Cell phones in China are even more popular than they are in the United States. There are actually more cell phones in China than in America. Many families have cell phones instead of wired phones.

Cell phones get consistently better reception in China than in the United States. The reason is that because China is an authoritarian state, reception stations can be put up at preplanned, optimal locations without negotiations or payments.

Measurement and Time Zones

Remember that the system of measurement used in China is the metric system. Length is by meters, speed is by kilometers per hour, liquid and dry measure is by liters, weight is by grams, area is by square meter, and temperature is degrees Celsius. For a chart to convert measurements between U.S. customary units and metric equivalents, see Appendix 13.

Since most of the world adheres to these standards, it is *we* as Americans who need to make the adjustment. It is also better if you carefully adjust your specifications to the metric system, rather than asking the Chinese to convert their measurements to the American system. If they are doing the conversion, many misunderstandings and errors can occur.

Time Zones

There is only one time zone for all of China. Also, there are no time changes for daylight saving time. China is approximately 5,200 kilometers, or about 3,200 miles, east-to-west, or roughly the equivalent of the continental United States. This means that at some times of the year in the western regions, sunrise and sunset may be much earlier than what you are accustomed to. Western Chinese compensate for this by changing their work hours. For example, normal office hours in Xinjiang Region, in western China, are from 7 A.M. to 3 P.M. Because national unity is an important objective in China, the policy of having one time zone probably will not be changed in the near future. These anomalies are not so great in the eastern part of the country, where you will undoubtedly spend most of your time.

The difference between Eastern Standard Time (EST) and the time in China is thirteen hours (twelve hours during eastern daylight saving time). That means 9 A.M. EST is 10 P.M. in China; 5 P.M. EST is 6 A.M. in China. Pacific standard time (PST) in the United States is fifteen or sixteen hours' difference. Remember that China does not have daylight saving time, so when we set our clocks back in the fall, the time difference will be larger by one hour.

Before calling China, be sure that you know what time it is there. We are used to time differences in the United States; if you're on central time and trying to reach someone on the East Coast during business hours, you know to call before 4 P.M. your time. Because the Chinese are not used to time differences, you must be sure to clearly explain them. When one American businessman started doing business in China, he gave out his home phone number to key people without enough explanation of the time differences. He got calls at all hours of the night. He then gave out twenty-four-hour clocks, which were set to his time zone, to repeat offenders.

Geography

When you make travel arrangements to China, or business appointments there, you are almost always dealing with the eastern part of China, or the southeastern and central parts. The map in Appendix 7 shows most of the cities that you are likely to do business in or visit. The government recognizes the vast western region as a huge untapped resource, and is especially eager to encourage investment and foreign capital in that area.

Whatever business you seek in China, it probably won't be in the west, unless you're looking for government assistance and concessions and want to make a sizable investment, or your business interests are agricultural or animal related. Keep in mind the reasons why concessions are necessary and forthcoming. In western China you will not have the industrial infrastructure that most industry needs—transportation access and the availability of complementary industry.

Population

Almost every city you will visit in China has a higher population than you anticipate.

See Appendix 10 for published population statistics. The Chinese people today are much more mobile than their parents were. Many rural people, especially the young, go to a city to make money and seek opportunities for advancement. Many workers are housed in temporary quarters, returning home only for holidays. They are not considered part of the population of the city they are working in and are not counted in the city population statistics. In fact, there are probably well over a hundred cities with a real population of more than 1 million.

A city like Shenzhen, for example, is listed at a population of 752,200. In fact, a closer estimate of the city's population would be about 3,000,000. Shenzhen has some residency rules that many workers cannot meet.

All of this makes for very unstable and misleading population statistics. Most statistics contain figures that are far smaller than the actual population totals, because they count only the city itself, not the surrounding metropolitan area, and don't count workers who do not consider their employment city their home, or who have not had their papers processed.

China has 105 cities with a population of more than 1 million. Other than Beijing, Shanghai, Hong Kong, Nanking, Xian, Wuhan, and several other cities, all the others are called "small" cities. These "small" cities have populations larger than our large cities. If a city has an airport, it is a "large" city by any American standard. If it has a train station, it is not small. You probably won't have dealings in any city that you would call small, but if you do, have your trip coordinator be very careful about your accommodations. Truly rural areas sometimes have extremely poor accommodations. There are many horror stories to substantiate that statement.

Chapter 8

Import/Export and Shipping Issues

You must decide up front, before you start this whole process of doing business in China, whether to negotiate using a third-party intermediary or just the help of a translator. Whichever way you go, the person communicating for you must understand the fine points of your situation and your objectives.

Using a Third Party: Trading Companies

If you decide to use a third party, your common choices are a trading company or a professional consultant. As with most things, there are benefits and problems with both.

Many people use trading companies to find sources. It is the quick solution for some of the problems discussed. However, there is a high cost for quick solutions. As in other dealings in China, it's important to know how long a trading company has been in business and the types of products they concentrate on. Many are state owned in whole or in part. Many people in such businesses do not speak English.

Trading companies have the same problems with sourcing, especially with relatively new sources, as you would have (see Chapter 9, "Finding Products and Partners"). If a company has not exported before, the trading company may not know of it. Because it is time-consuming and costly to find new sources, trading companies tend to deal with the same people over and over again. If the trading company is large, you may not get the attention or the quality help you need. If it is small, its contact list, available time, and knowledge of sources may be limited.

Trading companies negotiate prices and then negotiate with you at a higher price. They are middlemen. They perform a service and expect to get paid for that service.

In addition to the markup between the manufacturer's price and the price you will pay, they charge the manufacturer a fee for the shipping arrangements, typically between 1 percent and 3 percent. There is also a potential conflict of interest. Because the trading company takes markups and commissions, and may work with the manufacturer many times on an ongoing basis (whereas they may only work with you occasionally), its strongest motivation may not be to get you the best price possible, but rather to please the manufacturer.

Furthermore, trading companies usually take the easiest and quickest path and use sources they already know rather than take the time to understand your needs and make the effort to search for the best possible partner to meet those needs.

Also, trading companies are regionalized. Their contacts and sources are mainly in their own geographic location. Therefore, in order to maximize your chances of success, you need to know what area of China is best for the product you seek, before trying to find a trading company.

Choosing the right area is not as hard to do as it may be in the United States. Industry in China tends to be specialized and regionalized. Even government people can tell you what industries a city is known for, or conversely, which cities you should go to for a certain type of product.

You can get a list of trading companies from most American or Chinese government trade sources. If you've already chosen a region, check the local telephone books for listings.

One of the potential benefits of using a trading company is supposedly that it acts as an insurer. The idea is that the trading company, not the actual manufacturer, becomes your supplier. Money is paid to the trading company, and if the work is not performed or not performed properly, it is supposed to stand good for the money paid.

Unfortunately, it seldom works that way. Chinese firms in general, and trading companies in particular, are not customer-satisfaction-oriented or fond of refunding money or remaking product at an additional cost to themselves.

Expect to have trouble getting a trading company to make good for defective goods or other problems that would result in it paying out money. It will likely deny responsibility even when it has signed an agreement specifying what it will do in case the problem arises.

If you work with a trading company, your only contact with the actual manufacturer is through the trading company. Another downside is that it is much more difficult to establish close relationships with your source manufacturer when a middleman is involved, and close personal relationships are needed in any long-term relationship.

In summary, you may find it beneficial to deal with a trading company because it alleviates language difficulties, or provides you a quick method of sourcing, but do not count on that company as an insurer. In addition, be prepared to pay a premium for the company's services, and be cautious of conflict-of-interest issues. Most experienced Americans use trading companies only as an import/export tool.

If you still would like to work with a trading company, make sure you select the one that best suits your needs. First, you need to communicate well with the company. Make sure the agent comprehends your standards, exactly what you are looking for, what is acceptable and what is not, how tough you are on adhering to ISO standards, and what special skills are required. Find out also what experience the company's source has in making this product.

Before you get too particular, though, you should know that most agents in a trading company have no idea what detailed specifications look like or how to read an engineering drawing, so don't be surprised if you find that no matter what your standards are, they put you in touch with people who do not begin to meet your standards and whom they have not even met themselves.

Then apply other standard criteria to the trading company itself, such as the costs of its services, its resources, experience, attitude, and the scope and flexibility of the agreement. Bear in mind that as in any service business, the experience, competence, and authority of the actual person serving you is more important than is the firm itself.

Which decision to make depends on you. How much time can you afford to spend on sourcing? Can you resolve the language problem? How long-term is your need? If you have a one-time need for a specific product, or if the volume will be small, it probably doesn't pay you to do everything yourself.

If you expect a long-term relationship or very large volume, it may pay for you to incur the up-front costs to save large sums over the long haul.

Legal Issues

New and fast-changing laws and regulations will complicate your actions in China. Not only do you need to know the current law applicable to you, you also need to know the type and timing of future changes in those laws.

Among the notable legal changes is the release of the Expanding Import and Export Management Rights of FIEs rule. The rule now allows manufacturing FIEs to become export trading companies, which means they can purchase and export any products, free of quotas, license control, and government monopolies. This is the first step toward implementing China's commitment to liberalizing trading rights. FIEs in foreign trade zones are now allowed to establish offices outside the zones, which will enable FIEs to establish distribution networks across the country before the phase-in of the distribution rights. China's WTO accession promised a three-year phase-in of improved trading rights that improves conditions for foreign firms.

The Chinese government has moved to dismantle the near monopoly on import/export rights previously enjoyed by a few state-owned firms. Liberalization of the trading system was given major impetus in early 1999, when the government announced new guidelines allowing a wide variety of Chinese firms to register to conduct foreign trade. The guidelines allow, for the first time, both manufacturing and "non-production" firms to register for trading privileges.

Wholly owned foreign enterprises (known as WOFEs, which is sometimes pronounced "woofy") and individuals are still not permitted to directly engage in import activities, except to bring in material and equipment necessary for production.

As part of its bilateral WTO accession agreement, China committed to phase out many restrictions on trading rights. To meet these commitments, authorities are working on guidelines to allow foreign companies, subject to certain restrictions, to engage directly in trade. China has also agreed to gradually eliminate distribution restrictions.

Representative Offices and Import Documentation

Resident offices must submit a written application to Customs if they intend to import any personal effects or vehicles. Approval by Customs waives any relevant import license requirements and allows the office to import the equipment in reasonable amounts for office-use only.

As far as import documentation, normally the Chinese importer (agent, distributor, or joint venture partner) handles documentation requirements. Necessary documents include the bill of lading; invoice; shipping lists; sales contracts; an import quota certificate for general commodities (where applicable); import licenses (where applicable); inspection certificate issued by the General Administration of the People's Republic of China (PRC) for Quality Supervision, Inspection, and Quarantine (AQSIQ) or its local bureau (where applicable); insurance policy; and Customs declaration form.

All products sold in China must be marked—in the Chinese language—with the relevant information. AQSIQ requires imported and exported (but not domestic) food items such as candy, wine, nuts, canned food, and cheese to have labels verified and products tested for quality before a product can be imported or exported. According to the Food Labeling Standards of China, imported foods must have clear markings that indicate the country of origin in addition to the name and address of the general distributor that is registered in the country.

Import Tariffs and Customs Regulations

The most comprehensive guide to Chinese Customs regulations is *The Practical Handbook on Import and Export Tax of the Customs of the PRC*, compiled by the General Administration of Customs. This guide contains the tariff schedule and national customs rules and regulations.

When China decided to open the country to foreign investment, they wanted to do it in stages. First, in 1980, China established SEZs (special economic zones) in Shenzhen, Zhuhai, and Shantou in Guangdong Province, and in Xiamen in Fujian Province, and designated the entire province of Hainan a special economic zone. In 1984, China further opened fourteen coastal cities—Dalian, Qinhuangdao, Tianjin, Yantai, Qingdao, Lianyungang, Nantong, Shanghai, Ningbo, Wenzhou, Fuzhou, Guangzhou, Zhanjiang, and Beihai—to overseas investment. Then, beginning in 1985, the state expanded the open coastal areas, extending the open economic zones of the Yangtze River Delta and Pearl River.

Then, in stages, they kept adding more areas. As a result, a multi-level, multi-channel, diversified pattern of opening and integrating coastal areas with river cities, border and inland areas has been formed in China. As these open areas adopted different preferential policies, they not only developed the foreign-oriented economy, generating foreign exchanges through exporting products and importing advanced technologies, but also accelerated inland economic development.

The five SEZs are foreign-oriented areas that are primarily geared to exporting processed goods, integrating science and industry with trade, and benefiting from preferential policies and special managerial systems.

The Special Economic Zones, open cities, and foreign trade zones may offer preferential duty reduction or exemption. Companies doing business in these areas should consult the relevant regulations.

Tariff rates significantly lower than the published MFN (Most Favored Nation) rate may be applied in the case of goods that the Chinese government has identified as necessary to the development of a key industry. This has been particularly true of high-technology items. These products benefit from a government policy to encourage investment in high-technology manufacturing by domestic and foreign firms.

FIEs that produce certain types of high-technology goods, or that are export-oriented, do not have to pay duty on imported equipment that is not manufactured in China and that is for the enterprise's own use. China's General Administration of Customs has also occasionally announced preferential tariff rates for items that benefit other key economic sectors, in particular the automobile industry.

Foreign-Trade Zones/Free Ports

China's principal duty-free import/export zones are located in Beijing, Dalian, Tianjin, Shanghai, Guangzhou, and Hainan. In addition to these officially designated zones, many other free-trade zones offering similar privileges exist and are incorporated into economic development zones and open cities throughout China.

For detailed information about restrictions and other issues regarding exporting goods to China, use the Customs contact information here, or seek qualified expert advice:

The General Administration of Customs is divided into three sections:

Beijing Customs
Foreign Affairs Division
6 Jianguomenwai DaJie, Beijing 100730
Director: Mu Xinsheng
Tel: 86-10-6519-5243 or 6519-5399
Fax: 86-10-6519-5394
http://english.customs.gov.cn/default.aspx (site is in English)

Shanghai Customs—www.shcus.gov.cn
For English, go to *http://shanghai.customs.gov.cn/Default.aspx?tabid=4711* and in the upper right corner click "English."

Tianjin Customs—*http://tianjin.customs.gov.cn/default.aspx*
(no English site available)

Importing Costs
In determining costs and prices, keep in mind that freight, packing, and duty are part of the landed costs.

Freight Costs
Air freight is prohibitively expensive for any use except extremely valuable items, short-term perishables, documents, and samples. The largest commercial air carrier between the United States and China presently is DHL, which is especially used for heavy items. If you do not specify how to ship, the shipper in China will probably send it by DHL or by the China State Post Bureau (China Post). China Post still has most of the domestic courier market, although it has lost most of the international express-delivery-service market. Americans tend to use UPS or FedEx.

Our advice to clients is to use FedEx over the others. It is cheaper than UPS and is much better to deal with than the other carriers in case of tracking or other questions or problems.

The China Post is much cheaper, but the experiences many Americans have had with it haven't been good. It is slower, makes more mistakes, and its tracking is poor and not timely.

Container cost will vary widely depending on from–and–to locations and several other factors. A small container costs about two-thirds of a large container. Prices vary greatly by season, by port, and by supply and demand. Calculate the freight charges per unit and add that to the quote.

Planning the way you pack and ship can save you money. Sometimes, a cooperative manufacturer can lower your freight costs by packing differently, perhaps making cartons and packaging tailored to your product. Be sure to think three-dimensionally. Try to use all the vertical space you can. In some cases, freight costs have been reduced 30 percent by creatively designing the packing to best fit the product and the container.

Duty

Figure out duty beforehand, so you won't be unpleasantly surprised. If you are taking in a variety of products, know the cost for each category of product. Spend some time up front deciding a reasonable category for each product. For example, inexpensive jewelry could reasonably be classified as novelties. The duty on jewelry is 8 percent, whereas the duty on novelties is 3 percent.

Export Licenses

Determine whether your intended partner has an export license. The government grants export licenses, and only those with a license can export. If your partner does not have an export license, you will need to make some kind of deal with a trading company. This will entail an increased cost, but if you have sourced this company without a trading company, you will be in the driver's seat on negotiating prices with the trading company, since to them, this is extra or found money.

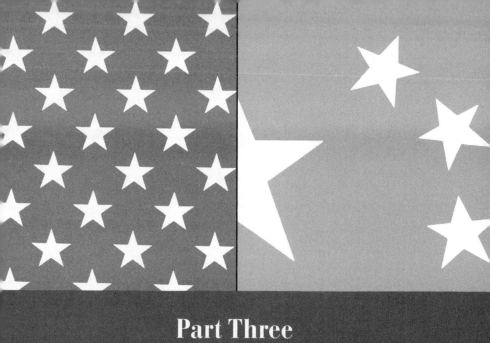

Part Three

Business Action Skills and Requirements

You will need the background and other information presented in Part One and Part Two in order to best utilize the "business action" chapters that follow. In order to do anything successfully in China you must recognize and know how to deal with the problems we've discussed up to now, as well as understand your counterpart's background and thought patterns.

Chapters 9, 10, 11, and 12 deal directly with the specific action areas you may be involved in when doing business in China. Chapter 9 deals with locating and selecting potential sources and partners. Chapter 10, simply put, contains what you need to know to establish a business in China. In Chapter 11, we'll delve into marketing your products in China, including advertising, distribution, and other marketing processes and the key considerations in selling products or services there. Chapter 12 takes up the process of investing in China, whether investing directly in a business or investing in asset value vehicles such as stocks and other financial instruments, and the investment options available to you. The last chapter in this section, Chapter 13, covers the essential topic of how to negotiate and close the deal, and follow it up afterward.

Chapter 9

Finding Products and Partners

SOURCING IN CHINA will not be as straightforward and standardized as you would like (as noted in the "Information and Statistics" section in Chapter 1). Putting aside the language, cultural, customs, and procedural problems, even if you were native-born Chinese it would still be a prodigious task to succeed at sourcing—except that if you *were* Chinese-born, you wouldn't have the same expectations of success in researching.

Problems of researching don't make it impossible to source in China, just more difficult. However, that can be an opportunity in disguise. The more difficult or complex a task is, the more chance you have to excel at it, with the requisite study and hard work. The difficulties are highlighted in this chapter in order to explain the reasons for the recommendations included for surmounting them.

Presourcing

As in performing any complex task, start by writing, in a concise and direct manner, exactly what your specific objectives are. Then think out and prepare how you will best present the benefits of your proposal to the people with whom you will be dealing.

China is much more of a networking society than is America. The Chinese are much more assiduous in maintaining personal contacts and in respecting personal referrals.

Therefore, if your reference to the contact was through a personal, not a public source, you should identify this fact to the person you are contacting. The more personal that your referral is, the better. It will help you in forming a bond prior to the negotiation stage.

Tell your Chinese counterparts briefly about yourself and your company—what you are looking for and what your sales expectations are. They are looking for potential growth in size, prestige, and knowledge, so if you have some technical expertise that they may learn, that's a big plus.

You will find that the Chinese don't have a high tolerance for working on-the-come; that is, taking risks without a clear understanding of the size and timing of the risks and rewards, and the probabilities of success.

Remember also that many of the Chinese lack experience and training in creative endeavors. The more precise you are—with drawings, specifications, pictures, and especially multiple samples—the more likely you are to get timely, meaningful answers. Write a precise proposal letter in English, and if you can, prepare a duplicate in Mandarin. Let your counterparts know that you have thought through this endeavor in depth.

Sourcing at Home

Get all the information you can from your home base. Start by using the Internet and by calling U.S. sources of information first. You will find U.S. sources very eager to help, especially if you are interested in exporting to China.

Then call information sources in China and get whatever information you can from them by phone. (See Appendix 16 for numbers.) You may need the aid of an interpreter to do this. Many people start by enlisting the aid of an outside interpreter and arranging a three-party conference call among you, your interpreter, and the party you are calling. Most multiline phones have this capability. Read your phone's instruction manual.

For calls involving more parties, you may need the assistance of a conference service, but these are quickly arranged and are affordable.

From the information that you gather at home, you can start to formulate a plan for your first trip. Make as many appointments as possible before leaving. Don't begin to try to set up a viable schedule until you get there.

Telephone Tips

Before you begin frequent calling to China, get into a low-cost calling program. Rates vary widely. You may pay as much as 40 cents per minute or as little as 4 cents per minute. One company, based in China, charges less than 4 cents per minute for calls from the United States to China.

If you set up with an inexpensive calling plan to China, it won't bother you so much to exhaust every avenue for finding information before traveling, even if some calls are time-consuming or unproductive.

If you are paper-oriented, write each piece of information on a different piece of paper or index card and sort by subject, but be sure to write a code for the source of the information on each item. If you are into computers, it's easier to sort and re-sort.

Do everything that you can from the United States, but don't dwell on it. You will get more information in China than you will here. Be prepared to travel to China before your major sourcing decisions are made.

Sourcing: Selective Methods

Let's talk first about the selective approach to sourcing, as opposed to what we call nonselective or bulk sourcing methods. *Selective sourcing* means working from a list which has already been preselected for capability, reliability, integrity, cost-effectiveness, and/or other factors important to you in a partner. This type of sourcing gives you reasons to believe that the sources chosen will be much better prospects for you than those you have rejected or others that you know nothing about. In America, we have several ways to do that, by networking, backward searches, and research, as described below.

Networking

Try to get recommendations from others who might be in a position to know, such as people who buy or make similar products, even if they are your competitors, or the supplier's competitors.

Backward Searches

Conducting backward searches means going from product to maker. Locate good-quality products similar to those you are looking for, and determine the maker.

Research

Research—finding information sources—may be close to bulk sourcing, but at least you can check certain facts before you contact a potential source. For example, you usually can find the source's sales volume, credit standing, capital resources, and length of time in business.

In China, selective sourcing for a foreigner works only in a limited way. Our first type of selective search is networking.

Certainly you will try to build a network once you're in China, but you probably won't have one to start with. Use every contact that you make to build your contact list. Ask your contacts whether they know of other factories seeking to export the type of product that you're looking for. Ask taxi drivers, hotel managers, other foreigners that you meet. Increased exposure gets increased results. You may be in the right place at the right time and find someone who really knows. I've acquired great leads from improbable sources.

A potentially significant recent development is the emergence of industry associations distinct from government agencies. If relevant, join an industry group and make a real effort to expand your network in that way.

A word of caution is in order here. When you ask Chinese people for a recommendation, they first think of who they know (friends, relatives, and so on) who might be available, not necessarily who would be the best for you. If someone gives you a personal recommendation for a company, supplier, employee, or partner, ask follow-up questions politely, such as, "How do you know this company (or person)?" "How do you know their competence?" Then analyze the response to determine whether you are being given a strictly personal reference or that your respondent really knows something about the competence of the person or company being recommended.

Sourcing: Nonselective Methods

If you are not satisfied with the results of your selective sourcing, you may have to fall back on bulk sourcing methods. "Bulk sourcing" is gathering data on a nonselective basis, that is, finding sources who may be able to fit your needs, but about whom you know little. You will list anyone who makes or might make what you are looking for, and then select a source based on inspection and interviewing techniques.

Methods of nonselective selection include information from telephone listings, government records, or sourcing based only on the location of the business.

If you do find that you must use nonselective methods, try to combine your findings with some selective methods, before you start knocking on doors.

The Canton Fair

To get in contact with companies who make the products you need, the most productive method is to attend shows and fairs, especially if you have difficult items to source, or specialized needs, or if you want to meet smaller firms. Those companies may not come to you, so you need to ferret them out and go to them. You may meet these people at small booths in shows and exhibits and by bulk sourcing techniques.

The granddaddy of all shows in China is the Canton Fair (now also called the Chinese Export Commodities Fair). Go there. It's a must if you're serious about doing business in China. The fair is located in Guangzhou in Guangdong Province. It started in 1957, and has grown and evolved ever since. There are now approximately 27,000 booths and 13,000 exhibitors at the fair, and it gets bigger every year.

The Canton Fair is held twice a year, from the middle to end of April and middle to end of October. Heavy industry is featured April 15 to 20; light industry, April 25 to 30. The schedule is the same in October.

The fair is absolutely the best place to find sources, especially for foreigners. These are firms that are ready and eager to do business with you, gathered all in one place for your convenience. It is relatively freeform. It is open to any firm anywhere in China with the money to pay for a booth and the desire to export. It is far and away the best place to meet face-to-face the key people in the most firms in the shortest period of time, all displaying their goods and ready to talk business. If you are serious about doing business in China, plan to attend. Plan your trip in detail and long in advance. Good accommodations are very pricey and hard to come by in show season. (See Appendix 11 for a list of recommended hotels.)

The fair is a great medium for sourcing for many reasons. Meeting the people who exhibit there face-to-face can tell you a lot about their attitudes toward you personally, customer care, and exporting; many people who are looking for products and partners discover that attitude is one of the most important elements in a solid and lasting relationship. The people who attend this event represent small companies as well as large. In almost any other method of sourcing, it is much easier to find large companies than small.

You may prefer a small company, especially if you are looking for a "captive" firm, where you are that firm's sole or majority customer. You may find that the largest firms with the best connections are not the best for you. They may be more protective than acquisitive. Also, larger firms tend to be somewhat arrogant. They do not realize that they have achieved past success in a relatively noncompetitive economic environment. Their prices and minimums may be too high for you, and their conditions may be too stringent.

China has only had a relatively free economy for less than twenty years. As fast as the amassing of capital has occurred, even large companies are relatively small by Western terms. There was almost no venture capital money available during that time, and very little private wealth. Therefore, growth and use of outside capital was hampered. Most money for expansion had to come from retained earnings. The lack of a burdensome tax structure certainly aided the amassing of capital, but still, dynamic growth was limited.

Especially in the early years, competition was limited to mostly government-owned businesses, which were not highly motivated; nor were they customer-oriented or competitive. Add to that the fact that China is a relational society and that most business was obtained on a negotiated and relational basis, not by an open competitive bidding system.

Firms grew in large part according to who they knew, and how well they took care of those relationships. Because competitive pressures were not nearly as intense as they are here, the need for efficiency wasn't as great. Cost-cutting techniques were not honed, especially in the area of labor. Larger and more prosperous firms did not necessarily become low-cost producers. They attained growth as a result of who they knew, not how efficient they were.

In some cases, Chinese firms developed the attitude that they can get all the profitable business they want and don't have to take risks or go out of their way for foreign business.

Many larger firms want to export more for the sake of image than for the desire to grow and improve.

If you want to meet smaller, hungrier up-and-comers, as well as the best of the larger companies, you will find many at the fair. Take business cards. And note that there is an admission fee to the fair. (For those without an invitation, the fee to a recent fair was 110 yuan, or about $14.)

To get there, one possibility is to fly into Hong Kong and take ground transportation into Guangzhou (car, train, or bus). Any ground transportation will take at least a few hours. Another alternative is to use China Southern Airlines, which flies direct from Los Angeles to Guangzhou. For help with travel arrangements to China, visit my company's Web site (*www.chinabusinesspartners.com*) or the show affiliate travel company's site (*www.icecf.com/en/service/travel_corp/index.htm*).

Either of these sites can arrange hotel accommodations for you. You also can go to *www.icecf.com/en/service/hotel/index.htm*; Appendix 11 lists the hotels found at that site.

Be flexible and make open plans for returning home, since you may find some companies worth pursuing and will want to make appointments to meet them at their factories after the show. Because of this eventuality, be sure to take enough cash and traveler's checks to extend your stay and to allow you to travel.

Discussion of going to the Canton Fair would not be complete without the usual warning label. Your biggest obstacle will again be language. Having a good translator with you will improve your odds of success by an order of magnitude. You can make arrangements for a translator prior to the show at a number of places. The two Web sites suggested earlier in this section for help with travel arrangements also arrange for or have staff translators. Though it's always best to have your own interpreter with you, exhibitors at the Canton Fair expect foreigners, so you will have a much better chance of having translators available there than you will anywhere else, should you be unable to line up a translator ahead of time.

Other Fairs and Exhibitions

The Canton Fair is separated from other business fairs simply by its size. No matter what products you are seeking, your odds of finding them are greater there. However, you should start with fairs and shows in general, since the smaller shows will get you acquainted with China shows and give you a flavor for the offerings and people. There are industry-specific fairs both in China and in the United States

Obviously, you will have a much better selection if you go to China, rather than waiting for the right show in the States. It's much easier and cheaper for the Chinese to exhibit in their own country. Also, the Chinese can have a hard time getting visas to come to America, whereas getting your visa to go to China is pretty much automatic. If a Chinese company does not already do business in the United States, getting a visa, even for a show in which it rents space, can be very difficult.

Hundreds of exhibitions are now held annually in China. Most are sponsored or cosponsored by government agencies, professional societies, or the China Council for the Promotion of International Trade (CCPIT).

Obviously, some shows are better than others, so ask specific questions when deciding which ones to go to. The number of booths, exhibitors, and visitors will give you some clues.

There are Chinese companies that attend industry shows in the United States, so if that is your preference, ask your trade association which of the shows are best for meeting Chinese exhibitors.

Bulk Research by Location

In addition to shows, there are other bulk sourcing methods. Unfortunately, they all require time, research, and language knowledge. First, the cities all have business license lists for businesses in their jurisdiction. If you choose an area you want to do business in, or one that is known for the type of products that you are interested in, get the business license list and sift through it. Again, you will need a translator. Most lists are not available in English.

The other bulk source approach is the telephone directory. That's the way most trading companies do it. Unfortunately, the directory will be in Chinese, so again, you will need some help.

These latter two approaches require that you start with a city and cull that city's lists. Both of these latter extensive research approaches are very time-consuming and require someone who speaks and reads Chinese. City officials are cooperative for the most part. Most behavior that you would deem unfriendly is caused by nervousness or the insecurity of having to communicate with foreigners and a lack of skill in English. When dealing with officials, make constant attempts to put them at ease. A smile goes a long way.

Since wage rates will be a major factor in determining the pricing of your products, check Appendix 12 for wage rates by key city.

Selecting a Source

There are several particulars to look for when selecting one source from a group of potential sources.

The first consideration is whether the source can do exactly what you want done to your satisfaction and within your time frame.

Many Chinese are enchanted by the idea of exporting to America. They tend to overreach their capabilities. They will try to do something, even if they don't have the experience, knowledge, expertise, or facilities to do it. You have to admire their spirit, but indulging their fantasies won't get you where you want to go.

Ask yourself what degree of certainty you have that they are capable—within your time frame—of successfully doing what you want done. They will say they can, but you need to look at the facts and decide for yourself. If they can't produce what you want, none of the other factors matter.

If they have the capability, then examine their attitude. Are they enthusiastic? Do they really want it? Attitude is important and can often overcome the inevitable problems. All potential partners are great when there are no problems and they are making money. You first learn the true character of your partner when there is a problem or a difficult deadline or a disappointment. You need to anticipate accurately how your partner will react. Most Chinese people want to dissociate from problems, even if it means the loss of the customer.

Does your potential partner understand the need for meeting both quality and time specifications? Does the company have adequate testing facilities? Does it appreciate the value of quality and reliability? Don't assume that a company knows what you know or that it has the same attitude about quality. Remember, the company earned its stripes when quality was not a major issue. Many Chinese companies still have difficulty truly comprehending all the implications of quality control. Most Chinese consumers have been used to thinking in terms of utility and price only.

Price is probably the biggest issue on your mind. You must bring the product in at your price point, but if you don't get satisfactory answers to the other factors, then the price won't matter.

On the issue of price, remember that even if a potential partner agrees to your price demands, your job isn't done until you can verify that it can sustain that price. Verify that the company's expenses are low enough to profitably sustain the agreed-upon price, and whether it will be able to control future expenses. Otherwise, you will find that whatever you agreed upon will change. You may have to dedicate your own people to teaching the Chinese company how to lower its expenses.

To summarize the selection of sources, consider the following criteria.

Capability
Does the vendor have the capability to do what you want done by the time you need it, taking into account experience, facilities, expertise, and resources?

Attitude

Does the vendor listen to your needs and comprehend them? Does it have the enthusiasm and attitude to carry you through any rough spots?

Quality

Does the company understand the importance of quality? If it does not currently have minimal testing facilities, it does not have this understanding.

Price

Is the company's price competitive? Will it be competitive in the future? Does it understand what makes a low-cost producer?

Depending on what you are after, other considerations may be important, such as these next ones:

Creativity

Creativity might be one of these extra points. Most of the Chinese are not used to thinking outside the box. You will find it extremely difficult to get good creative work done. They have lived in a regimented society. They're not used to being given flexibility. Freedom of thought is a new concept, but many can be very creative with the proper guidance.

Younger people are usually more flexible, but I've found some real gems in older creative people. It's as though they were waiting for an opportunity to express themselves. In bringing out creativity, you need to make it clear what the guidelines are, or explicitly tell them of the absence of guidelines and define the important objectives.

Region

It is always difficult and sometimes very misleading to generalize about anything. However, there seem to be differences by region in the way people do business, their practices, beliefs, and ethics. Just as New Yorkers, Southerners, and Midwesterners have certain practices and attitudes attributed to them, the Chinese have stereotyped the reputations of their regions.

Of course, it's a dangerous practice, and many good firms can be overlooked in this process, but for a firm new to China to conduct the selection process, it may help to focus on an area. Most people in China know of the regional reputations; if you are so inclined, ask business people, banks, and government officials about a region's reputation before you focus on an area of study.

ISO Certification

Some companies, mostly larger ones, have established a certain level of ISO certification as a criterion for selection. In China, there are ways of purchasing ISO certification without having fulfilled the actual ISO requirements. Also, there are companies that understand the need to obtain legitimate certification as well visually impress foreigners. They may invest in construction, equipment, and space, meeting the letter of requirements, in order to get certification and pass muster with plant auditors, without ever having met the spirit or true meaning of the requirements. In other words, they institute whatever is needed to get business and then operate as usual, never having fully comprehended the reason why certifications and audits are important and meaningful.

Does this negate the benefits of ISO? Not at all. It's just another warning flag to you to keep focused on what you're really looking for. You want good quality control that does not allow bad product to be released; adequate control of the in-process system, which facilitates the quick identification and discovery of the source of any problem; and solutions that fix the root causes of any problem rather than just the symptoms. You may use ISO certification as a criterion, but make sure that the ISO concept is actually practiced and embodied in the factory's day-to-day work.

Factory audits

Factory audits are mandatory. You must see where your goods will be made, the equipment that will be used, the test procedures that will be used, and everything else that is relevant to your orders.

You will encounter situations in which a manufacturer tells you that he makes certain components, when actually he buys them. Obviously, this difference has major consequence when making decisions about the manufacturer's capability for future products or quotations. During the inspection/audit process, be sure to stay focused on the basic, important issues. Concentrate on the entrée, not the garnish.

Make sure that product not up to specification won't go out. Make sure that the manufacturer's process is such that he will find and correct problems quickly and permanently, but make allowances for how he accomplishes that.

Appearances aren't as important as actual results. Remember that in the Chinese environment, equipment and first-class facilities are often more expensive than labor. We are trained to think in terms of saving labor costs wherever possible. To us, labor is almost always the most expensive ingredient. To the Chinese, labor is often the least costly ingredient.

One of our largest and most well-known manufacturers went sourcing for an important component of its product. Domestic production quality was good, but prices had increased to a point that the manufacturer felt it had to find a less expensive source. After sampling and quotations, the company narrowed down its selection process to four possibilities—two in China, and one each in Taiwan and Korea. Our client settled on the Korean source.

We became involved a year after that decision. The manufacturer had a serious quality issue that had not been resolved in that length of time. We started by researching the original selection process. Although the Korean quote was somewhat higher than that of the Chinese firms, and the

Korean samples not as precise, its paperwork was excellent and its plant facilities and equipment were new.

We spoke to one of the engineers who had done the physical inspections. Although the samples of one Chinese manufacturer were consistently perfect, that company had not filled out the questionnaire properly, nor did it have impressive facilities. In summarizing his comments on why he did not recommend the company, he closed by exclaiming, "and one room had a dirt floor!"

We spoke to that Chinese manufacturer and determined that its attitude was good, but it had produced several samples of different products, each of which required planning and special fixtures. The manufacturer was not paid for its efforts, although it pulled people from fulfilling paying orders. Also, it was not fully informed of the process or what was at stake.

We suggested that our client give the Chinese manufacturer paid trial orders, subject to close inspections until the company proved itself. The Chinese manufacturer committed to improving its facilities if assured that it would be getting substantial orders. Making an exception to the selection rules proved a Herculean task, until one executive finally pointed out the obvious: the current situation was not tenable. A change had to be made if the objective was to be met. The exception was made, and the trial was successful.

Chapter 10

Establishing an
Operating Company

WE HAVE ALREADY touched on the topic of choosing a location for sourcing a partner in Chapter 9. The same statements can be made here. Since industries tend to be regionalized in China, it may be advantageous for you to consider being in the same area as other firms in your industry. Some of the reasons for doing this are the ability to hire personnel experienced in your industry, with the skills your industry may require; easier access to support industries and suppliers; and customer expectations. Other considerations are ease and cost of transportation, wage rates, and proximity to key customers. Weigh all these factors and any others that are important to you before determining the area in which to locate.

Be sure to check the reputation of the government in the zone that you might choose. Some are much more helpful and flexible than others. Other companies located in that zone—especially other American companies—will usually give you a heads-up on that.

This decision has an impact on the registration and licensing time and cost and occupancy costs. Economic-zone management people have government-owned facilities for rent or sale, or can direct you to where to look for facilities.

Registration and Licenses

If you are starting a business in China, you have many more hurdles to overcome than you would when starting a business in America, and many more points to bear in mind. As you probably would guess, the registration process is far more complex than it is in the United States, although the Chinese government is making a sincere effort to make it somewhat simpler and easier. For one thing, China's new Company Law has reduced the amount of minimum registered capital.

It's a good idea to plan extra time into the process, because you will probably encounter unexpected delays. Also, budget more money than you can easily foresee needing. One use for extra money is for entertainment, lunches, or small gifts to facilitate attention and conversation.

One factor that makes the process more confusing is this: In America, we seek precise language to make sure that there is no ambiguity in laws, regulations, and procedures. This precision is not found in China, which results in a lack of what might be called legal transparency—rules, laws, and procedures that are clear and unambiguous.

In China, most things are open to interpretation. You may interpret something one way and the government official whose approval you need may interpret it differently. Furthermore, if you see three different officials about the same problem, you may get three different interpretations.

Obviously, you want things interpreted in the way that is most beneficial for you. This requires real knowledge and skill. This job is best left to people who are experienced and have been successful in dealing with government people in the past. When you do have contact with government officials, remember not to show your frustration or anxiety. Smile and be pleasant.

Depending on your business and what licenses and favors you need, you may see as many as ten different bureaus, agencies, and ministries. Plan your strategy and priorities up front, ideally with someone experienced in this process.

Before you begin to deal with government agencies, you need to have a physical address and a local bank arrangement set up, with access to enough funds to pay for whatever fees you will need. The banking connection you have could be a source of early information about the process. Depending on whether you build, buy, or lease your facility, you will have contact with government officials and businesspeople who will also be sources of information about the licensing process.

If possible, also seek guidance from someone in the same line of business who has gone through this process successfully. Even that may not help as much as you'd like, though, because the Chinese do not value precedents as much as Americans do. Therefore, no matter how the other firm succeeded, you may still have to find a different path.

When you are ready to start the licensing process, write down what you need for each license or permit and make sure to draw up a critical path plan so that you get what you need from one agency before you get to an agency that requires it.

Be prepared for setbacks. Losing a battle doesn't mean that you've lost the war. With the help of an expert, you can craft a different strategy or approach.

Murphy's laws will surely be in operation. You'll encounter problems that even experienced people did not anticipate, and it will take you longer than your worst-case scenario, but eventually, you can succeed.

As mentioned before, most Chinese like Americans. That goes for government people also. Small gifts that are distinctly American (Chinese-English dictionaries, American flag pins made in America, American museum souvenirs, sporting goods, T-shirts, movie and other posters, and so on) will do you a world of good.

Wholly Owned Foreign Enterprises

Some companies prefer to establish a WOFE, rather than a joint venture, with a view to retaining greater management control; this may be due to concerns over intellectual property rights (IPR) protection, desire for simplicity, or for other reasons of corporate policy.

There is a strong trend toward WOFEs in China now. Firms that are just now starting up favor it, and firms that started as joint ventures out of necessity are reverting to it with the liberalization of the laws. The main reason that many foreign firms chose to form joint ventures with the Chinese was that when foreign companies first entered China, there were policy restrictions on foreign investors in many Chinese industries.

The law on WOFEs requires that they either provide advanced technology or be primarily export-oriented, and it restricts or prohibits them in a number of service and public utility sectors. This is changing dramatically, though, and now, as a practical matter, you can set up your business as a WOFE unless you antagonize the authorities.

An increasing number of U.S. companies find a WOFE to be a viable entry vehicle to the China market, taking much less time and money to set up than a joint venture.

American companies should bear in mind that joint ventures are time-consuming and resource demanding, and will involve constant and prudent monitoring of critical areas such as finance, personnel, and basic operations in order for them to be a success.

China's Company Law

China's Company Law, which has been in effect since July 1, 1994, permits foreign companies to open branches. As a policy matter, China still restricts this entry approach to selected banks, insurance companies, and accounting and law firms, but this is scheduled to change. While representative offices are given a registration certificate, branch offices obtain an actual operating or business license and can engage in profit-making activities.

In order to encourage foreign investment, foreign companies were given tax breaks that allow them to pay less than domestic companies. The standard corporate tax rate in China now is about 33 percent, but foreign companies typically pay less than 15 percent. Under a new plan, foreign companies in China before the end of 2006 will pay the current rate until 2011. The new plan calls for phasing in tax increases in five years, perhaps starting at about 24 percent and gradually increasing until domestic and foreign companies pay the same rate.

Establishing a Representative Office

Establishing a representative office gives a company increased control over a dedicated sales force and permits greater utilization of its specialized technical expertise. The cost of supporting a modest representative office ranges from $250,000 to $500,000 per year, depending on its size and how it is staffed. The largest expenses are office rental, personnel housing rents, expatriate salaries, and benefits.

Establishing a Chinese Subsidiary

A locally incorporated equity or cooperative joint venture with one or more Chinese partners, or with a WOFE, may be the final step in developing markets for a company's products. In-country production avoids import restrictions—including relatively high tariffs—and WOFEs provide U.S. firms with greater control over both intellectual property and marketing.

Operations Purchasing

Under new laws, foreign-invested enterprises (FIEs) retain the right to purchase equipment, parts, and raw materials from any source. Chinese officials, however, still encourage localization of production. Investment contracts often call for foreign investors to commit themselves gradually to increase the percentage of local content. All things considered, when planning your venture it's probably a good idea to commit from the beginning to sourcing locally when possible. Then you can make that point clear throughout the negotiation and start-up phases.

Technology Licensing

Technology transfer is another initial market-entry approach used by many companies. It offers short-term advantages but runs the risk of creating long-term competitors. Due to this concern, as well as intellectual property considerations and the lower technical level prevailing in the China market, some firms attempt to license older technology, promising higher-level access at some future date or in the context of a future joint-venture arrangement.

Licensing contracts must be approved by and registered with the Ministry of Commerce of the People's Republic of China (*http://english.mofcom.gov.cn*). A tax of 10 percent to 20 percent (depending on the technology involved and the existing applicable bilateral tax treaty) is withheld on royalty payments.

China has agreed to implement the Agreement on Trade-Related Investment Measures (TRIMs) upon WTO accession. China has also committed to enforce laws or provisions relating to the transfer of technology or other know-how only if they are in accordance with WTO rules on protection of intellectual property rights (IPR) and TRIMS.

Personnel Concerns

FIEs can integrate a joint venture partner's work force, hire through a local labor bureau or job fair, advertise in newspapers, or rely on word of mouth. Representative offices are required to hire their local employees through a labor services agency.

Many Chinese employers pay less than minimum wages, which are $50–$70 per month in coastal factories for about 50 hours of work per week. Workers who are sick, injured, or pregnant don't get help from their employers. Labor law enforcement remains lax to make it more attractive for investment. In second-tier jobs, clerks make $100 per month for 50–60 hours plus room and board and three meals including meat and vegetables.

Skilled managers, especially those with marketing skills, are often in short supply, although many companies have found an abundance of talented and highly motivated recent university graduates. Experienced managers in FIEs command salaries greater than their counterparts in Chinese enterprises, making localization increasingly expensive for many companies. However, it does give them a greater choice of qualified top-level people. Many top people prefer to work in an American company. They believe it offers them better salaries and benefits, increased opportunities, and better training. Also, being alumni of an American company makes them more marketable should they decide to leave.

Finding and keeping competent engineers and technicians can be difficult. Shortages of skilled labor are, at times, especially acute in south China due to the relative scarcity of institutions of higher learning in that region. Some recruiting for plants in south China takes place in northern regions. Many workers prefer the climate and the higher-class social environment in many southern regions.

Hiring and Retaining Employees

At non-supervisory levels, workers tend to be less motivated and somewhat less productive than an average American worker. One problem encountered in dealing with the Chinese worker—which can be turned into an opportunity—is that his expectations are low. He isn't expecting to be in one job very long, and he expects to be easily expendable. He takes the job for money. The Chinese employer attitude is that labor is cheap and doesn't require much attention.

Some American firms have taken advantage of that attitude by paying attention to their Chinese workers, laying out careers instead of short-term jobs, and raising the pay level somewhat above the average. Those actions can raise the productivity level and instill loyalty.

If you are planning on expanding your work force, tell workers about job opportunities and encourage them to bring their friends and acquaintances to you. This gives them the image of being important and is a big benefit for them.

For middle and upper management, money is not now the top reason for taking a job. The potential to grow and to have a close working relationship with their superiors are now the most important reasons for job change at that level.

To get top talent, you need to be prepared to coach your hires, to be their mentor. Products of the one-child rule tend to be pampered and need personal attention.

Americans usually believe that bosses shouldn't get into employees' personal lives, but many of the Chinese today want just that. For example, a common problem that employees seek help with is how to gain independence from their parents. The workers look to understanding bosses to help them with such problems.

Chinese workers are now far more mobile than their parents were in terms of moving residences and employment. They feel far less loyalty to their employer than was previously the case. At upper levels, younger Chinese employees today typically don't stay in one job for more than two or three years, unless they have an exceptional relationship with their superiors and feel comfortable with their progress. They are looking for training and fast advancement.

Once your enterprise is established and your key people hired, you must constantly work on cementing their loyalty.

In addition to the tried and proven methods that are part of your core business in the United States, you can maintain your employees' loyalty by giving them personal attention and constant exposure to new ideas, increasing their participation in the parent company, and letting them know that they are known and appreciated by the key people in the parent company.

You also have the ability to offer some benefits that local firms cannot. Trips to America for your key people and their spouses are a major incentive. Also, bear in mind that the Chinese have a deep desire to provide benefits to their children.

You can offer a visit for an employee's child, or, even better, arrange for the child to study in the United States. Some schools are actively seeking students from China; if you were to act as intermediary and the child were to be accepted, your employee would be morally bound to you.

Your selection of the chief executive in China must be the right one, because he needs to have great autonomy and the immediate ear of his superiors for major actions. Executives in China need greater authority of action and autonomy to accommodate the need for faster action on larger issues. If they need approval from bosses not completely familiar with the issues in China, and who demand more and more information before giving their approvals, the executives will lose the important ability to act in a timely fashion.

Your Chinese supervisors and executives are more likely than your employees in America to take an action on their own that is counter to company policy or philosophy, because they are much less likely to fully comprehend and embrace company policies. They still must have the autonomy to make decisions and do the job quickly and efficiently, but they will need much more timely supervision than do your people based in the United States.

Also, keep in mind that a decision that you would make in the United States may not be the best one to make in China. So before countermanding what your executive in China wants to do, be sure you understand his reasons and be flexible enough to allow his logic to persuade you if it has merit.

Many times American companies work hard at setting up their Chinese subsidiary, staffing it with good people, and equipping it properly, and then forget that keeping their people connected and identified with the company is a continuing job.

Problems in maintaining loyalty are great. They are the same ones that made your task of setting up the business in the first place so daunting. Language, customs, and culture make it difficult to keep everyone in the business connected.

On the other hand, you have some benefits that local companies do not have. Working for an American firm has greater prestige.

Compensation

Workers may be paid a salary, hourly wages, or piece-work wages. (See Appendix 12 for average relative wage rates.) China's national labor law also requires compensation for overtime work. Because it is common to provide subsidized services, such as housing and medical care, compensation beyond the basic wage constitutes a large portion of a venture's labor expenses. However, with increasing availability of mortgages and financing of more purchases, this nonmonetary portion of compensation will decrease, as fewer workers will need employer-furnished housing.

Chinese executives expect an extra month's pay for the Chinese New Year, and lower-level people expect monetary gifts at that time as well.

Local governments also require enterprise and worker contributions to pension and unemployment insurance funds. Tax rates for pension funds may run as high as 20 percent of an enterprise's total wage bill.

Employees must also contribute between 3 percent and 8 percent of their salary as a withholding tax to the government, depending on the locale. In general, FIE ventures are free to pay whatever wage rate they choose as long as it is above the locally designated minimum wage.

In practice, income-tax laws often make it desirable to provide greater subsidies and services rather than higher wage rates. Most FIEs determine their methods and calculations of salaries and benefits after observing local practice.

Management and Specialty Training

China lacks executive training. Its current managerial class lived in the era of Mao Zedong and came of age in a planned economy. Very few have had formal training in the management skills required in a market economy. Until very recently, their only experience in an evolving market economy has been competition against competitors who also lacked experience in a market economy. Furthermore, since the government wanted to nurture the burgeoning entrepreneurial class, China's own managers were given many advantages over foreign competitors. Their main competition, therefore, was against other Chinese managers in a relational society, where knowing the right people was more important than possessing modern managerial skills.

In 2002, the government officially launched an MBA program at thirty universities, aimed at training executives who can build and manage companies in a market economy. These programs are very pricey and are attended mostly by people who are already top executives. These graduates are highly prized and command much higher salaries. It is China's first step toward building a domestically educated managerial class.

Large Chinese companies are now recruiting Chinese employees overseas who were trained in foreign companies and in respected Western universities. The companies feel they can entice top talent away by offering a better advancement program and closer ties.

Those companies are meeting some success, since foreign Chinese feel that a glass ceiling exists at foreign multinational companies that prevents ethnic Chinese from progressing upward. Foreign Chinese in who work in Chinese companies have some feeling of belonging, as well as more autonomy and freedom of action, without the need for approval of home offices in other countries. Perks in Chinese companies are fewer, but pay can be competitive, and often an extremely favorable stock or option deal can be worked out. Another consideration for some is to have an impact on the country, helping in its transition.

American companies have the opportunity to hire Chinese-Americans who have the advantage of speaking both Chinese and English and feel more at home than non-Chinese-Americans. Chinese-Americans who are fluent in the language can speed-read reports and regulations. Since most records are kept by hand, penmanship and the ability to read and write Chinese can be a very important advantage. Another advantage is that native Chinese people often find it easier to approach Chinese-Americans than other Americans.

Termination of Employment

The ability to terminate workers varies widely, based on location, type, and size of enterprise. Terminating individual workers for cause is legally possible but may require prior notification and consultation with the local labor bureau and labor union. In general, it is easier to fire workers in southern China than in the northeast, and in smaller enterprises than in larger ones. FIEs do not encounter problems letting workers go who were hired on short-term contracts at the end of the contract period.

Employment of Host-Country Nationals

Rules for hiring Chinese nationals depend on the type of establishment. Although FIEs are not required to employ Chinese nationals in their upper management, in practice, expatriate personnel normally occupy only a minority of managerial and technical slots, most being held by Chinese nationals.

However, if your company is just starting out in China, plan on having some key American personnel in China, even though you may be planning on hiring all Chinese nationals for the top spots, until certain preset objectives are met and the local team is deemed ready to run on its own.

This is the most common mistake that smaller companies make. They do not have the high-level executive manpower to spare and they treat their China operation as they would a U.S. branch. Don't open in China until you are prepared to devote the supervision it will require. That supervision includes the kind of financial controls that will give you the ability to prevent misuse or financial misunderstandings; assure the inculcation of your company's core values, beliefs, and policies; assure that they are comprehended and accepted; and above all, enable you to implement a communications system that allows for effective supervision in the future.

In some ventures, there are no foreign personnel at all. The Chinese respect authority. If they can deal with Chinese people who are in top positions in your enterprise, they will feel comfortable. If, on the other hand, all of your top people are expatriates who do not speak Chinese fluently, you will lose a great deal of goodwill.

American companies must do a better job of motivating good American employees to work effectively in China, instead of treating their time there as a temporary prison sentence.

Japanese and some other foreign businesses in China seem to succeed more often than do American businesses. There are several reasons for this. The Japanese send dedicated, experienced people to work in China, and there are many incentives for them. In China they have their own cars, whereas back home they may have ridden the subway. They have more living space, better housing, more luxury in general, and a wealthier image.

In contrast, most Americans are reluctant to go to China because they perceive hardships and a downgrade in lifestyle. They see relative isolation for their families, problems in education for their children, many fewer entertainment options, difficulty traveling, difficulty getting the products and foods they are accustomed to, and so on.

Operations Concerns: Transportation, Training, and Ethics

On several occasions, I've mentioned that our experience in America leads us to make assumptions in China that are not true and cause difficulties. This is very true in the operations area as well. This section will help you prepare yourself for problems in China that you otherwise might not even have thought about before getting there.

Americans seldom think of the utilities needed to run a business. The assumption is that basic utilities are available when we need them. You may be unpleasantly surprised in China. Getting enough power during your operating hours may not be a consideration in the United States, but in China, it is a major problem. Power may be shut down for parts of a workday or even for days at a time. Check the power experiences in your area before you begin. Also, find out if any rate increases are planned, as well as the rate history. One American company that is a heavy power user budgeted costs carefully, only to find that a short time after opening, power costs increased by almost 30 percent.

If you need water, check the quality before you open. Many times, American companies find that it is polluted beyond any acceptable level. Also, if you are locating where heating your building is a factor, check your source of heat.

A very common problem in China is locating suppliers that you find acceptable. Some American companies make the mistake of assuming they will find competent local suppliers, only to find that the local firms do not make what the company needs, or cannot produce what is needed within the company's tolerance range. Check out your suppliers carefully before you commit yourself.

Also check the dexterity and skill of the average local worker in doing the things necessary to produce your product. Basic workers are not as experienced at some things as an average American worker. Don't assume that basic workers have been exposed to common tasks. One company that hired many workers on a daily basis found that the local workers had never seen a pair of scissors. You need to know about unpleasant surprises more than pleasant ones, but one pleasant surprise some companies have had is finding that local workers have certain arcane skills that far exceed those of American workers.

Also, for most monotonous work, Chinese workers may be superior.

Domestic Freight Transportation

China's logistics present another obstacle that is often underestimated. Although China has improved its logistics dramatically, there are still major problems getting goods from point A to point B in a cheap, efficient, reliable manner. It is estimated that transportation costs are perhaps 20 percent more than in developed countries relative to product costs.

Several major problems remain with China's transportation system. First, the nation has not fully completed its highway network, and delays are commonplace. Another problem is that regulations are neither consistent nor coordinated and the regulations that are in place are not transparent, or uniformly enforced. Some local officials impose certain fines or restrictions, even banning certain vehicles from traveling through their territory. Also, because of lax enforcement, some vehicles are so grossly overloaded that they cause safety hazards, accidents, and delays.

The government is aware of these problems and is in the process of addressing them by coordinating the activities of the various agencies involved, and cracking down on local abuses.

Although not required to by WTO agreements, China will allow foreign companies to operate wholly owned road transportation companies this year and to own fully coordinated freight-forwarding companies providing full-line services by the end of 2006. This will increase competition and, it's hoped, improve many of the logistics industry's ills.

These problems with intra-China freight make freight to customers and from suppliers a real consideration in location planning.

Technical Training

Once you have hired your key personnel, start technical training as soon as possible. Provide experts from your company and from the equipment manufacturers, if that would add significantly to the training quality. You must have translation services available during training, and you should encourage questions. Strive to produce the same quality product in China that you do in the United States.

Business Ethics

You need another kind of training also, which may be far more difficult: training in American business ethics. Many practices are endemic in China that you would find downright dishonest or unethical, and would be grounds for dismissal in the United States. In general, your Chinese employees will believe that if you haven't adequately protected against certain behavior, you are allowing it.

Purchasing people commonly take kickbacks from their sources. Their sources are not dealt with at arm's length. Using relatives and friends as suppliers is also common. Expenses are padded and phony receipts are widely used. Basically, the cost of all goods and services purchased by your employees that is compensated or paid by the company is inflated.

There are two things you must do to prevent these abuses. First, every new employee must receive indoctrination in company ethics. Outline the behavior that you expect, explain why it is necessary, and set the rules for violations clearly, making certain practices punishable by reimbursement by the violator and immediate dismissal.

Second, you must have safeguards built into your operation rules that protect you against this behavior. Inform every supplier and bidder that the company will eliminate the services of any supplier who is found to have contributed to kickbacks or falsified receipts. Also, institute an anonymous tip system, with all tips going directly to your chief executive.

You must also compensate your purchasing people significantly more than average, to make up for the money they would have ordinarily made on kickbacks.

Chapter 11

Marketing in China

STARTING AT THE TIME when China was beginning to open to the world, many people tried to market products and services there and failed. It became axiomatic that while America was a consuming society, China was a producing society. This is no longer true. Finally, China is becoming the consumer society that everyone thought it would be.

As more businesses open, more people, wanting to share in the prosperity of the cities, move to metropolitan areas from the countryside. The factors of a burgeoning economy, the usual circumstance of having both husband and wife employed, and the one-child rule have created much more discretionary income, leading to a growing middle class. As well as a producing society, China is in the process of becoming a consuming society.

Consumerism in China

At this time, China's distribution system is not yet fully developed. Also, the limited size of the average retail outlet, the difficulty of retail transportation, the lack of uniformity of goods carried, and the lack of public information media mean that consumers have limited success in finding particular items. Depending on what items the consumer is looking for, he probably won't know where to buy exactly what he wants.

The lack of credit cards and established consumer loan procedures are also hindrances in growing the consumer segment, but these shortcomings are also being addressed. Credit card issuance has been increasing and is approaching the steep part of the bell-shaped curve.

The consulting firm of McKinsey & Company has agreed with many others who predict that China's credit-card industry will experience some dynamic growth very soon. They estimate that more than 15 million credit cards have now been issued in China, the great majority in the last three years. They predict that consumer credit will be one of the fastest-growing segments of the banking industry, with the top two products being mortgages and credit cards.

Retailing is still dominated by small stores and stalls, with very limited selections, but this is changing as some giant retailers such as Wal-Mart and France's Carrefour are successfully opening superstores. Many independents will be forced to expand or die. As mobility increases, more people are able to reach major shopping centers.

Now that China is in the midst of a consumer revolution, foreign products are leading the way, complete with advanced marketing, advertising, and research techniques. Brand awareness is increasingly important, and sophisticated advertising is beginning to play a crucial role in charming the Chinese consumer. Foreign products are expected to continue making inroads.

Retail sales of consumer goods are now more than RMB 5 trillion ($625 billion USD), and are rising at a rate of about 12 percent a year. Even so, the developed countries, and especially the United States, are pressing China to encourage consumer spending, pointing to the global trade imbalances. China had a $200 billion trade surplus with the United States in 2005.

At around 50 percent, China has the highest national savings rate of any major economy in the world. This compares to the savings rate in America of about 2 percent.

As people have become more prosperous, their spending has not increased proportionately to their earnings. Consequently, most of their increased earnings have gone into savings. It is now estimated that China has well over $1 trillion in personal savings, compared to about $158 billion in the United States, and that savings has quadrupled in the last six years.

A great portion of the savings is deemed to be precautionary. China does not have a government health-care system, or a real pension system. So, there is much that the government can do to change the mindset of the Chinese consumer: protecting against life's uncertainties, lowering personal income-tax rates, and facilitating private insurance plans. In fact, the government has shown interest in encouraging spending.

As disposable income grows, China's market potential expands. The combination of WTO, the liberalization of rules, government incentives, and an expanding economy bode well for U.S. sales in China in the years ahead and America's ability to penetrate this market.

China has already become a real contributor to sales and profits for many American companies. For example, some time ago the U.S. company Corning was hit with a 16 percent tariff on many of its products made in China because it allegedly was dumping. Corning says this has resulted in a decline in Chinese sales that has been so steep that it offset gains in both North America and Europe.

Corning's case illustrates China's growing influence in the international tech industry. Once just a manufacturing center, China has become the place to develop and sell high-tech goods. It's the industry's greatest hope for growth this decade.

Plunging into the market can pay off. Corning's sales in China have jumped 80 percent since 1998, to $134 million in 2003. China is Oracle's fastest-growing market. In its 2004 fiscal year, Dell sold 60 percent more PCs to China than it did in 2003, making that country Dell's fourth-largest single-country market.

U.S. trade groups say that there remain obstacles to unfettered U.S. sales. There are still many laws favoring Chinese suppliers, especially in the government sector. In addition to laws, there is biased interpretation of rules, as well as customs. Emphasis on proprietary standards in purchasing slows innovation and gives unfair advantages to Chinese companies who own the proprietary standards specified.

China has reasons to want its own standards. Technology royalties can be very expensive. Makers of DVD players have to pay as much as $22 to the coalitions of companies, including Toshiba, Sony, and Time Warner, that developed the technology. Considering that some DVD players sell for under $40, that's a big bite.

China sometimes changes the rules of the game when it sees a chance to develop domestic technology to lessen its dependence on foreign technology.

China is trying to get into product design, especially for its domestic market and also to sell its own brands elsewhere. China now is designing cars, and it is already the fourth largest car market in the world. When China puts together a good consumer credit and finance program complete with rules, regulations, and protections for creditors, that market will explode. Although Chinese consumers have been used to buying whatever was available, they do have their own tastes and are now demanding products that cater to those tastes.

Many foreign manufacturers are hiring and training Chinese employees to create future designs in cars that are more in tune with Chinese tastes and habits. One custom that could make for differences in popularity and sales is that many businesspeople have professional drivers for business driving, but want to drive their cars themselves on weekends and off hours. Also, many extended families are buying cars for use by the whole family. The Chinese make much more use of the rear seats than do Americans, and the rear passenger areas need to be larger and afford more privacy.

As stated before, everything in China is changing. The country is moving in favor of free trade and open competition, which could benefit astute American competitors.

Advertising

One of the ramifications of the move from a state-owned economy to a free economy is the need for differentiation leading to a growing emphasis on advertising. Because China was accustomed to products made by state-owned firms, there previously was little differentiation or brand consciousness. When brands were introduced and differentiated, the Chinese became brand conscious. Today, they are very brand conscious.

In keeping with this is an advertising explosion, a phenomenon that will continue to grow. With state-owned businesses, factories only had to meet production quotas and send the output to another entity to market. Since there was little competition, there was no need to advertise, or any reason to establish brand recognition.

Now that competition has increased, advertising is an effective way to create product awareness among potential consumers in China, as it is here. Channels for mass advertising include publications, radio, television, billboard displays, Internet, and sports sponsorship.

China's retail boom and the increasing competition among retailers are making China's advertising industry grow even faster than the economy as whole. Already, all of the major international advertising firms are present in China.

Chinese restrictions within the advertising sector include requirements for the verification of safety and hygiene from the relevant ministries that monitor various consumer products. Censorship standards vary considerably throughout China. Once again, good relationships with these ministries help.

Television advertising takes the largest single portion of the Chinese advertising market. China's regular television-viewing population represents 84 percent of China's 1.3 billion people.

The Ministry of Commerce (formed in 2003 by merging the Ministry of Foreign Trade and Economic Cooperation [MOFTEC] and the State Economic and Trade Commission

[SETC]) is now the primary regulatory organization for the advertising sector, but many other organizations, such as the Ministry of Culture and the State Administration of Radio, Film, and Television, play an active role in controlling what ends up in print or on television.

National Marketing

Many of the future events in China can be predicted from America's own past. One of the economic processes going on in the United States is the consolidation of industries. A greater and greater percentage of sales in most industries is being concentrated into fewer and fewer firms. Even industries that were textbook examples of free competition dominated by small firms in the United States, such as farming and retailing, are now somewhat advanced in the process of consolidation.

There are many advantages and disadvantages to consolidation, but it is a fact of modern economic life. Advancements in communications, availability, cost structure of national advertising, and many other factors have contributed to this trend.

There are now clear signs of the consolidation trend in China, but the trend is too new to have yet resulted in truly national firms in many industries. Look for this trend to continue with vigor and to have an increasing impact on you and your business in China.

At this point, if you are trying to put anything together on a national basis in China, you will have to deal region by region, but this will change over the next few years, as some firms will come to the fore in many industries. The need for nationwide transportation, advertising, warehousing, and distribution to enable firms to conduct national campaigns is being addressed by aggressive firms and the easing of government impediments.

Given China's size and diversity, as well as today's lack of agents with wide-reaching capabilities, it makes sense to engage several agents to cover different areas, and to be cautious when giving exclusive territories. In statistics and studies, most reports divide China roughly into at least five major regions: the south (Guangzhou), the east (Shanghai), the central/north (Beijing-Tianjin), the northeast, and west China. Perhaps a more logical breakdown of China's regions in the future, considering the fast growth of inland areas, would be the north (Beijing-Harbin), the east (Shanghai), the south (Guangzhou), the central (Xian), and west China; or possibly a sixth region could be created by calling Beijing-Tianjin the north central region and adding a northeast region (Changchun-Harbin).

Before China's accession to the WTO, China prohibited foreign companies from distributing imported products. China is liberalizing its distribution system to provide full distribution rights for U.S. firms.

Providing and Obtaining Services

China's service sector has been one of the most heavily regulated parts of the national economy—and one of the most protected. Without quality service nationally, it is difficult to sell anything nationally, but as stated before, this is expected to change soon. The service liberalization included in the bilateral WTO agreement will dramatically improve foreign access to this sector.

The Chinese economy itself will benefit from the increased scope of services, professionalism, and technologies that foreign investment in services will bring. There will be substantial efficiency gains in the domestic economy also, resulting from increased foreign participation in financial, insurance, telecommunications, distribution, and professional services, as well as after-sales service and repair businesses.

Foreign companies were normally not permitted to directly provide after-sales service and customer support for their products sold into China, but FIEs can now provide such services on products that they sell in China.

Foreign firms sometimes engage authorized Chinese entities to provide service, often on a contractual basis, or to establish service centers jointly that can provide both spare parts and after-sales service. American companies have complained that such arrangements give them inadequate control over the quality of customer service and result in the loss of customer confidence. Some companies have opted to provide regular service from bases outside of China, such as Hong Kong.

Direct Sales

Major U.S. direct-selling companies entered the Chinese market in the early to mid-1990s, when China's legal and regulatory framework for this industry was not very clear. Direct selling was quickly copied by domestic Chinese companies, some of whom abused this legitimate format of doing business and operated scams to rip off consumers and evade taxes.

In early 1998, the Chinese government started implementing a series of strict controls over this industry, culminating in the relicensing of all direct-selling companies. Although a few major U.S direct-selling companies were reissued their business licenses, the restrictions were severe and the requirements many, resulting in a difficult business environment.

There has been a loosening of these restrictions for legitimate businesses, and recently China's State Council approved long-awaited rules on direct sales that lift the ban. This opens the market for TV sales of such items as cosmetics, health-care items, and nutritional supplements.

E-commerce

The Chinese government has adopted an open attitude toward the advent of electronic commerce in China. Interest among both Chinese and international businesses focuses on investing and establishing vertical integration and sales channels online.

Investment is risky, however, due to the lack of clearly defined regulatory powers over the industry, an effective Chinese certificate authentication system, secure and reliable online settlement system, and an efficient physical delivery system. Many American IT sector companies have been actively engaged in jointly developing these systems in China. WTO accession should increase the speed of these developments.

The rapid growth of the Internet raises interest in using e-commerce in China. Though China remains a developing country, the ambitious use of high technology has made inroads in government and industry.

The SAIC's (State Administration for Industry and Commerce) in some economic zones have begun a licensing process to create a "reasonable and reliable market," despite the lack of credit card usage and the distribution difficulties. Many firms have already been granted licenses to sell online advertising.

Most Chinese consumers are sensitive to price and will usually choose the less expensive product. For big-ticket items, favorable financing arrangements provide a great boost to sales.

Chapter 12

Investing
in China

IF YOU ARE THINKING of investing substantial money in a
facility in China, you will need the help of good Chinese
partners and qualified consultants with solid government
knowledge and contacts, especially if anything requires
government approval. Don't go to the government for
anything without the help of people who know and have
worked with the government and have established government contacts.

As much as the government may want your investment,
it is extremely partial to giving special privileges if Chinese
nationals are involved, or if the government is convinced
that the country as a whole will benefit.

This used to be the exclusive domain of the Ministry of
Foreign Trade and Economic Cooperation (MOFTEC), but
since 2003, when the Ministry of Commerce was formed by
merging the MOFTEC and the State Economic and Trade
Commission, the oversight of investments has been decentralized depending on what it is and where it is. If in doubt,
contact the Commerce Ministry.

Decisions are greatly influenced by national policy, but
the decision-making is surprisingly decentralized. Relatively
important decisions are made by relatively low-level officials, putting much more importance into the value of your
knowledge, contacts, references, and relationships.

Enterprise Investments

China remains the leading developing-country recipient of foreign direct investment (FDI), although FDI actually dropped in 2005. Hong Kong's investments in China outpaced investments by other economies because Hong Kong's entrepreneurs were willing to accept the risks of investing in developing China before other investors were. As China's WTO entry makes the operating environment more transparent and predictable, however, Hong Kong's role will change. Shanghai is emerging as a major alternative to Hong Kong, although the limitations on convertibility of the Chinese currency will impede Shanghai's ability to overtake Hong Kong.

Most foreign private equity investments in China are actually housed in offshore investment entities, which, as with other offshore FDIs, can be transferred without Chinese government approval.

A large number of firms have opted to channel their investments in China through vehicles registered in three tax-haven economies: the free ports of the British Virgin Islands, the Cayman Islands, and Western Samoa.

On a cumulative basis, the United States is the second-largest foreign investor in China, after Hong Kong, and ahead of Japan, Taiwan, and other countries.

Although the WTO is primarily concerned with trade, China also took on obligations to eliminate certain trade-related investment measures and to gradually open opportunities for foreign investment in specified sectors that had previously been off limits. New laws, regulations, and administrative measures aimed at implementing these general and sector-specific commitments are being issued at a rapid pace. Prospective U.S. investors will want to examine carefully the particulars of these new measures as they emerge.

Encouraged, Restricted, and Permitted Investment

China attempts to guide new foreign investment toward "encouraged" industries and regions. Over the past five years, China has implemented new policies introducing new incentives for investments in high-tech industries and in the central and western parts of the country in order to stimulate development in less developed areas. The government has a catalog that lists sectors in which foreign investment would be encouraged, restricted, or prohibited. This catalog took effect April 1, 2002, replacing the December 1997 list. Unlisted sectors are considered to be permitted.

According to an accompanying regulation, projects in "encouraged" sectors benefit from duty-free import of capital equipment and value-added tax rebates on imports. The same regulation states that approval authority for "restricted" investments rests with the relevant central government ministry and may not be delegated to the local level. Practically, though, if you can obtain a recommendation at a local level and have good contacts at the central government ministry, it might work to your benefit to make your request at the local level first.

Investment Incentives

China has developed and expanded a complex system of investment incentives over the last twenty years. The Special Economic Zones (SEZ) of Shenzhen, Shantou, Zhuhai, Xiamen, and Hainan, as well as fourteen coastal cities, hundreds of development zones, and designated inland cities, all promote investment with unique packages of investment and tax incentives. In recent years, the areas not included in previous SEZ lists, wanting to join in China's prosperity, have now set up their own zones. The result is that you may now feel free to go to most areas, whether officially listed or not, and try to work something out.

The great majority of FDI has been directed to China's coastal provinces. Since 1979, 86 percent of cumulative FDI has gone to the eleven provinces and provincial-level cities along the eastern and southern coast. Nearly two-thirds of cumulative FDI receipts have gone to just five provinces:

Guangdong (27.9 percent), Jiangsu (12.8 percent), Fujian (9.5 percent), Shanghai (8.3 percent), and Shandong (6.2 percent). Of these, FDI to only two of the destinations grew faster than the national average in 2001: Shanghai (up 35.8 percent) and Shandong (up 18.5 percent).

All five areas have been particularly targeted by manufacturing firms based in Taiwan and Hong Kong, attracted by low labor costs for export production. Shandong has also been especially popular with Korean firms.

Keep in mind that the statistics presented here will not be representative of the future, since investment currently is already expanding more rapidly in the interior than in the listed areas.

China announced special investment incentives to attract foreign investors to its highly underdeveloped central and western regions. Individual provinces have also issued their own additional incentives.

Foreign investors sometimes have to negotiate incentives and benefits directly with the relevant government authorities. Some incentives and benefits are not conferred automatically. The incentives available include significant reductions in national and local income taxes, land-use fees, import and export duties, and priority treatment in obtaining basic infrastructure services.

Chinese authorities have also established special preferences for projects involving high-tech and export-oriented investments. Priority sectors include transportation, communications, energy, metallurgy, construction materials, machinery, chemicals, pharmaceuticals, medical equipment, environmental protection, and electronics.

The investment climate and business environment in the more rural areas are significantly less sophisticated and more arbitrary than in the coastal areas, making it difficult for foreign investors to assess prospective investments. Talks conducted vis-à-vis should help clarify the attitude of the authorities, the enthusiasm for your project, and specific incentives.

FDI in China continues to flow overwhelmingly to the manufacturing sector. Two-thirds of FDI went into manufacturing projects. In the initial phase of China's economic opening, manufacturing FDI was concentrated in low-technology garments and other soft goods. Starting in the 1990s, however, China also began receiving growing amounts of capital-intensive (chemicals and petroleum processing) and technology-intensive FDI.

The two fastest-growing sectors for new FDI are electronics and communications equipment (up 54 percent) and textiles (up 40 percent), demonstrating that China continues to gain competitiveness in higher-technology products without giving up its dominance of low-end manufacturing.

With the exception of real estate, service-sector investment has been minimal, mainly due to Chinese government restrictions. The ratio of manufacturing to service investment should dramatically shift toward service over the coming several years as China phases out current barriers affecting foreign access to service industries as part of its WTO accession agreement.

China encourages reinvestment of profits. A foreign investor may obtain a refund of 40 percent of taxes paid on its share of income if those profits are reinvested in China for at least five years. Where profits are reinvested in high technology or export-oriented enterprises, the foreign investor may receive a full tax rebate. Many foreign companies investing in China have adopted a strategic plan that reinvests profits for growth and expansion.

Mergers and Acquisitions

China's inadequate merger laws and policies and the absence of property-rights guidelines have posed substantial obstacles to foreign mergers-and-acquisitions (M&A) activity in China. A simple share buyout can occur under existing regulations, but it would be subject not only to the approval of all partners in a given venture but also to that of the supervising Chinese government agency. The Chinese government is now approving a growing number of such deals. (Note: Foreigners may purchase shares in a small minority of Chinese companies listed on Chinese stock exchanges, but foreign portfolio investment is currently restricted to less than majority ownership.)

Regulations in this area are being liberalized, though, and government sentiments are toward modernizing China's Company Law to accommodate more inter-country mergers and acquisitions. If you have interests in this area, make sure that your information on restrictions is current, since it is changing rapidly.

Regulations and periodic updates on China's investment projects and conditions can be found by contacting the Commerce Ministry.

If you are examining the books of a potential merger or acquisition, please look at the balance-sheet comments made in Chapter 13 in the section titled "Rules For Negotiating."

Securities Law

The Securities Law, which went into effect on July 1, 1999, codified and strengthened the administrative regulations that govern the underwriting and trading of corporate shares, as well as the activities of China's stock exchanges. The government has now passed new legislation designed to toughen penalties for insider trading, falsifying prospectuses and financial reports, and other forms of fraud. The Securities Law does not distinguish between state-owned enterprises (SOEs) and non-SOEs.

Capital Markets and Portfolio Investment

The development of China's domestic capital markets has not kept pace with economic needs. Two stock exchanges have been established—one in Shanghai (in November 1990), and one in Shenzhen in southern China's booming Guangdong Province (July 1991). Other regional "securities exchange centers" have been closed by the China Securities Regulatory Commission (CSRC).

The CSRC lacks experienced personnel and has turned to the United Kingdom and other countries for more training. China's stock markets are gradually adopting accounting standards closer to those in use in other markets. Again, the practical advice here is don't trust anything having to do with stock investments without verified, firsthand knowledge.

Insider trading is rampant, and accounting standards are not nearly what they are in the United States (and even ours are sometimes suspect).

Although FIEs, in theory, may apply for permission to raise capital directly on China's stock and bond markets, the approval process is difficult. In the case of shares, the CSRC has indicated that it plans to treat FIEs the same as domestic firms. As a practical matter, though, it will be several years until raising capital in China in this manner is a viable alternative capital resource.

With provisional regulations that took effect September 1, 2001, China permitted the establishment of foreign-invested venture capital firms, including WOFEs, but the firms are limited in scope to encouraged and permitted high-technology sectors.

Until recently, American investors trying to participate in China's growth and opportunities have largely bought the small number of Chinese stocks that trade on U.S. exchanges, investing in American Depository Receipts (ADRs), the domestically listed shares of Chinese companies, or China-concentrated mutual funds. This number has been increasing of late, with sixteen Chinese companies being listed on NASDAQ in the eighteen months prior to September of 2005 and more prospective listings being applied for.

Other options for American investors are now emerging. China-focused exchange traded funds (ETFs), such as Powershares, USX China Portfolio, and others, which track an index composed of U.S.-listed Chinese stocks, offer some protection because American markets are so heavily regulated. Today there are many ways for an American investor to invest in China at various levels of protection.

Standard and Poor's raised China's overall credit rating to A- from BBB+ in the last half of 2005.

Knowing the Risks

Before getting into the details of various investment alternatives, keep in mind that investing in China is not like investing in the United States, with the only difference being that the companies are located in a different country. *Investing in China is much more risky.* Even the least-risky investments in China are more risky simply because they are in China and your ultimate recourse—a legal remedy—has to be played out by Chinese rules, at great expense to you, with murky laws.

As you get into the alternatives that require investment through foreign companies, remember that foreign firms, especially Chinese, are not usually as customer-oriented as most American firms. News about any customer complaints doesn't travel as far or as fast as it does here, nor does it have the same impact.

Also, you must make a judgment about the reliability of information about Chinese companies gathered by other parties. Has your information source gathered his own information firsthand, and how reliable and competent is he?

If you are risking a meaningful amount, either be very sure of your information source, or go to the company itself and do your own research.

The number of scams regarding mainland Chinese stocks are legion. As mentioned above, insider trading is rampant, and accounting standards are not nearly what they are in the United States. As a rule of thumb, Chinese companies keep multiple sets of books (see the discussion of accounting practices in Chapter 6) and prefer to give ambiguous answers to direct financial questions.

If you are still not discouraged and would like to do some preliminary research, check out some Web sites that were listed in a *Wall Street Journal* research report (see Appendix 15).

The sections that follow outline some of the investment alternatives, with commentary on their characteristics.

ADRs

ADRs and other U.S.-listed Chinese stocks that trade on the New York Stock Exchange and the NASDAQ stock exchange are the easiest to buy and sell, and offer the most complete information, because those companies must adhere to U.S. generally accepted accounting practices.

The problems are that the selection is limited and that, by some accounts, they have been bid up way beyond the prices they would carry for comparable companies in the United States, simply because the number of Chinese companies easily marketable is so limited. Furthermore, many of those firms are formerly state-owned companies that do not have the same growth potential as do the more entrepreneurial companies.

Mutual funds and ETFs

Mutual funds and ETFs own a broad range of Chinese stocks, offering investors diversity to buffer a disaster in any one stock. Of course the flip side to diversity is that super-performance of an individual stock is buried in the whole.

Actively managed funds usually own a selection of Hong Kong–based stocks, Hong Kong–listed Chinese-company stocks, and ADRs. Some own "B" shares of Chinese companies trading on mainland exchanges.

Mutual funds with major holdings in Chinese stocks in Hong Kong and China include Mathews China Fund and U.S. Global Investors China Opportunity Fund, both of which have performed well in recent years.

"H" shares and Red Chips

"H" shares are issued by companies incorporated in China, and Red Chips are shares issued by companies incorporated in Hong Kong. Both are traded in Hong Kong. These fall under the aegis of Hong Kong's securities regulators. Since Hong Kong regulation is far stricter than Mainland China's, it provides a stricter financial reporting structure.

Since Hong Kong was turned over to China by the British in July 1997, it has formally been part of China. The Chinese government has pledged to allow Hong Kong to remain independent. For the most part it has kept that pledge, with some notable exceptions, mainly in the political area.

As long as the government remains totalitarian, it will brook no serious challenge to its form of government, or to any of its main objectives. The government's direction, rules, and regulations can sometimes be mercurial. Therefore, the degree of autonomy Hong Kong will have in the future is at least a question, which raises another question about the superior regulation that the central government now has over Hong Kong–listed stocks.

In terms of securities regulation, though, Hong Kong retains much British influence and is more sophisticated and tighter than China, which has had a history of loose regulation. Still, Hong Kong is significantly less strict than America, and in legal practice it still tends to favor Hong Kong's people versus foreigners.

Investing overseas is a higher risk, but if that is your direction, there are brokerage firms, such as SHK Financial Group and Boom Securities in Hong Kong, that will open accounts for American investors online or by e-mail and offer online trading. There are more Chinese company listings in Hong Kong than on any other exchange outside of Mainland China.

Hedge funds

Hedge funds themselves are a significant risk without the added risks of stocks in a market like China's. They are poorly regulated and can follow a much riskier game plan, including short selling, than do mutual funds and ETFs.

Also, hedge funds usually have very high minimum investment standards and typically take fees that are a percentage of assets, as well as taking a percentage of profits.

"B" shares

"B" shares are shares in Shanghai- and Shenzhen-listed companies that foreigners can buy. They are priced in Hong Kong and American dollars. They are more risky than Hong Kong–traded issues because they are not subjected to the same strict regulation, and the shares may be difficult to buy or sell. On the other hand, this is where you will find the smaller entrepreneurial companies with the highest growth potential.

"A" shares

"A" shares are not available to foreign investors, but they represent most publicly available (called "published") stocks of Chinese companies. However, along with all the other liberalizing steps the government is taking, it is changing foreign restrictions to investment in "A" shares. For example, UBS AG is allowed to purchase up to 800 million "A" shares on behalf of foreign retail customers. UBS is not particularly small-investor friendly, but more steps toward allowing foreign investment in "A" shares are planned.

"A" share companies are proposing plans to float their non-tradable shares and are offering compensation to holders of tradable shares. The most popular offer is more shares. Also, some "A"-share firms are proposing alternative plans, such as "company buy backs," cash dividends, and stock-price protection against price erosion. The plans need a two-thirds majority of stockholders to pass.

In 2004, China's Commerce Ministry loosened regulations on Chinese companies investing abroad, which led to Chinese foreign investment rising in 2004 by 27 percent, to $3.6 billion.

The China Securities Regulatory Commission took steps to bolster the stock markets, now near eight-year lows, including approval of buy-back programs for companies to reduce the number of outstanding shares, and allowing certain shares of listed companies not traded to gradually change hands.

Despite concerns about the political uncertainty, a shortage of entrepreneurial and managerial experience, and controls on foreign capital, China has received a surprising amount of seed money from U.S. venture-capital firms. There were forty-three deals recorded in 2004, totaling $557 million, almost double the amount of money invested in Indian ventures. U.S. venture-capital accounts for almost half of all venture money from all nations.

Lack of Transparency of the Regulatory System

China's legal and regulatory system still lacks clarity, precision, and consistent enforcement despite the promulgation of thousands of regulations, opinions, and notices affecting foreign investment. Although the Chinese government has simplified the legal and regulatory environment for foreign investors in recent years, China's laws and regulations often are still ambiguous.

Foreign investors continue to rank the inconsistent and arbitrary enforcement of regulations and the lack of transparency as two major problems in China's investment climate. No prospective foreign investor should venture into the China market without considerable firsthand due diligence plus the advice of trustworthy and knowledgeable professionals.

Real Estate Investing

Since Beijing has allowed private ownership of property, real estate has become a hot alternative investment medium.

Official statistics show that prices rose some 90 percent in the last four years to what amounts to an average of $800 per square meter (or about $74 per square foot), making it already unaffordable to most prospective Chinese buyers. In

Shanghai, the prices of homes rose a sharp 26 percent in 2004, and slightly less in 2005, according to official numbers, which are probably understated.

Therefore, one Chinese problem seems to parallel one of our current problems. China is worried about a housing bubble, especially in the large commercial centers such as Shanghai.

Just as in the United States, there is much speculation, with people buying real estate for investment purposes rather than for living in. Foreign investment is also present, adding to the price push.

China is very anxious to avoid a bust, which has happened in the past to several Asian cities, including Tokyo and Hong Kong. The government is very sensitive to any problem that might cause civil unrest. Any price collapse in real estate might also cause a banking crisis. Although mortgages only account for somewhat over $300 billion in bank loans out of a total of $2.3 trillion, most other loans are collateralized with property.

The government, attempting to avoid a price collapse, has targeted Shanghai as a critical point in fighting this phenomenon and has instituted a 5.5 percent capital gains tax on housing sold more than once in a year.

Beijing is prepared to do a lot more if need be, but there are already indications that prices may be cooling.

Chapter 13

Negotiating and Afterward

Most Chinese have specific views on foreign trade, foreigners in general, and Americans in particular. Again, these are generalizations, and not all people in China have the same views.

Chinese people have selective attitudes toward foreigners. You may be surprised to learn that most Chinese businessmen like to deal with Americans more than any others. This is a generalization and depends on individual experience and other factors, but is mostly true.

The Chinese (the people, not the government) specifically picture themselves as straightforward, which is why they relate best to Americans, whom they picture as also being straightforward. The opinion of the majority of businesspeople is that most Americans say what they mean and mean what they say and are not out to cheat them. Most Chinese businesspeople have friends or relatives who live in America or have visited here, and they admire us. It is a distinct advantage.

There is a hierarchy of general opinion. Japanese are liked the least. Swedes and the English are nearer the top, while Germans and Turks are nearer the bottom. That does not mean to say that the Chinese won't deal with those they like least. You will see that they deal with Japanese, Germans, and others extensively, because those foreigners typically are more aggressive, but Americans do have the initial advantage.

Understanding Your Counterparts

The Chinese like to deal with Americans partly because of our "good guy" image, but unfortunately, also partly because we are more trusting and can be deceived more easily. Many Americans, when dealing with the Chinese for the first time, see the naiveté of the Chinese in some matters, and assume that they are too naive to be able to take advantage of Americans. That is not the case.

The great weakness of Americans is our self-image of superiority and our desire to help and to teach American ways to others. The Chinese will often capitalize on those feelings.

Chinese-Americans are most vulnerable to losing money in China, because they think that because they speak the language and understand the heritage, they have an advantage. If they have assimilated American values, however, this false sense of confidence can be a big disadvantage.

We Americans do have a negative side to our image, but few of the Chinese will mention it. The adjective to describe this side of Americans is "arrogant." Many Americans think they're superior, and they show it. Some large American companies have advanced that image by acting as though the world should bow at their feet to do business with them. Many times, they have been harmed by that attitude.

An American manufacturer says something like, "We are General Widget. We are the largest maker of widgets in the world. If we accept you, you have a chance of getting constant orders for millions of pieces." Then it asks for samples and quotes. If the samples are good and the quotes are acceptable, then the Chinese manufacturer expects orders. Instead he gets volumes of paperwork in English, which he will have great difficulty filling out and which require a commitment of days of time to complete.

If the paperwork ever gets completed to the American customer's satisfaction, then the customer's engineers visit the Chinese factory and give a detailed report of all the items that need to be fixed or changed. No factory I have seen, no matter how new or well organized, has passed one of an American multinational corporation's inspections without a list of to-do items.

While this process is progressing, there are requests for the manufacturer to do special extras or tooling, which is expensive for him, without any compensation. At one point or another, many Chinese manufacturers bow out of the whole process, saying that they have paying customers to serve.

Chinese manufacturers cannot figure out why they must go through that much nonproductive work, if they demonstrate their ability to make a better product, cheaper than the customer can get elsewhere. Their view is that it is a form of insult. The customer is saying that it is a big American firm and the inferior Chinese firm will do anything to work with them. Of course, you cannot put your trust in a Chinese firm simply because it made a good sample and quoted a good price. However, you should understand its point of view. The Chinese company doesn't have the money, the need, or the training to pursue potential orders when the process seems to have no end. Also, forms submitted in English without interpretation or explanation make the Chinese firms very uncomfortable.

If a manufacturer is deemed to be a good potential supplier, show some goodwill by paying at least some of the cost of samples and special requests, explain in some detail why the company must go through this due diligence stage, and give it some support in filling out the necessary paperwork. Just your understanding will go a long way toward building goodwill. Some Americans are arrogant. Don't be one of them.

Foreign trade is exciting to most Chinese. Businessmen who are into foreign trade are held in higher regard by their peers and by the government. Since the Chinese are very image-conscious, and foreign trade gives them prestige, they want to pursue the concept.

Because the possibility of the Chinese doing foreign trade is a relatively new phenomenon, they appear to know more about it than they do. Don't assume that they are well versed in the details, especially if they do not engage in foreign trade regularly.

The image-consciousness of the Chinese may also surface during your negotiations. Always remember that the Chinese people must appear important to you and others.

For instance, you may face a situation where you visit a factory only to find that it is a small, slab building in a poor area and that the owner and his family sleep in the back, but the owner nonetheless tells you that his minimum order is more than you are willing to place.

Don't react by taking a hard line and pointing out the obvious. If you are still interested in dealing with this supplier, give him the image he is seeking. Treat his demands as legitimate negotiation points and negotiate a lower minimum, while respecting his "image" need.

Many exporters were cheated in the early days, and tales of those experiences have circulated, making some of those businesspeople very cautious in their dealings with foreigners. They need to feel comfortable with you. References and facts about your business and accomplishments will help.

Members of your party should show deference to the senior member of your own group. The Chinese expect it. Emotions and facial expressions should be tightly controlled. We tend to express emotions as facial expressions. The Chinese do not, and they don't like people who express displeasure, annoyance, or impatience openly. They take it as a sign of immaturity.

As you get into the substance of how to negotiate with the Chinese, bear in mind the topics that were taken up in earlier chapters, since many of the points made previously in this book will enter into the negotiation process.

Rules for Negotiating

Before entering into negotiations, you must do extensive investigative work and follow some very important rules to ensure your own survival.

Rule 1: Make certain that your project is independently economically viable.

Profitability of a project or the sale of goods and services should be based on sound economic criteria. Do not rely on promises of subsidies, incentives, special considerations, or non-market-related sources of income to create a profit. If incentives are offered, they should be used to augment profit, not create it.

Rule 2: Know your partner. Do your "due diligence," and do it well.

Be sure you know what *their* objectives are and who is the head of your partner's team. Be sure that your negotiating counterpart has the authority to make a decision.

Make certain that your potential partner is not a shell subsidiary of a larger company. If the partner defaults, do you have the ability to collect from the parent company? Specify this in your contract. Remember that the best contracts are those that do not have to be enforced; that is, both partners have the same motivations.

If you look at the balance sheet and other financials of Chinese companies, you will probably see a heavy reliance on short-term debt and very little bond or long-term debt. This is common in China and stems from traditional bank lending practices, past government regulations, and normal Chinese financial management, which has been relatively unsophisticated and lacking in long-term planning. Such a circumstance is customary in China, and should not be viewed as especially egregious management.

Rule 3: Establish ground rules at the outset of negotiations.

Keep minutes. Be prepared for protracted negotiations, especially with state-owned enterprises. Negotiations with state-owned enterprises or with government officials is different from that with private companies. The former does use Sun Tzu's *The Art of War* tactics.

Rule 4: Don't make assumptions regarding your potential partner's intentions.

The thought processes of your Chinese counterparts are different from yours, their objectives are different, and their background and experiences are different. It is probable that their assumptions are also different. Make sure that your partner comprehends the nuances of what *you* want. If there is any doubt at all, ask your counterparts to explain their understandings in their own words.

Rule 5: Search for problems before they materialize.

In addition to creating pro formas, spend some time at the beginning of a project to create scenarios of what you will do if things go wrong. Try to anticipate possible problem areas. If you can't find any, you are not looking hard enough.

Create a strategy to deal with potential problems. Know your limits on losses as well. Be sure to limit your exposure. Set milestones in the project for performance. Have an escape strategy for each stage of the project if milestones are not met. Seriously question any agreement in which you are told you can ignore or avoid the law.

Rule 6: Get paid.

A contract with an insolvent partner or customer is worthless. Pay careful attention to how you get paid, when you get paid, and in which currency. Never agree to unsecured payments after delivery.

Hidden Problems

Here are some hidden problems that most foreigners don't know about. They are very important, and will affect your negotiations.

Accounting

As bad as some of America's more spectacular violations of generally accepted accounting practice standards have been, the point is that we do have detailed, logical account-ing standards. Most Chinese businesses do not. As mentioned earlier, it is common practice in China to keep at least three sets of books—one for taxes, one for operations, and one for the owners or investors.

No matter how good the Chinese might be in hands-on operation of a business, they do not yet comprehend modern cost accounting, nor do they attach overhead in an objective, life-of-product manner.

Therefore, you will find that if you want them to manu-facture any style, model, or product that they have not made before, or do anything that requires procedures they have not used before, or to manufacture to different specification standards or use equipment that they do not now own, they won't have an objective, practical, long-term way of deter-mining how much it will cost.

The lack of objective information encourages a large fudge factor, which will tend to push their quoted prices beyond what their true costs would suggest.

Your production may be assigned a heavier share of the overhead than it deserves. Furthermore, the usual mindset of Chinese businesspeople tends to make them believe that as time goes on they are much more likely to be forced to cut prices than allowed to raise them. Add to this their lack of experience at using incremental costing or power costing to gain market share, and you may find that their price quota-tions are on the high side.

The flip side of this coin is that if you are costing a prod-uct that they have made for some time, they may tend to be on the low side, since they figure that much of their invest-ment and learning costs have already been recovered.

Risk Analysis

You might assume that the Chinese have infinite patience and a long-term point of view. That was the case with the older generation, but it is not so much the case with the younger generation. When it comes to the "return on investment" type of issues, or returns of goodwill and other intangibles, you will find the Chinese myopic. They understand the principles of cream skimming very well, but they do not normally believe in taking even temporary losses for long-term gain.

Modern American business is more and more often calling upon sophisticated risk-analysis techniques. It is now an "in" subject, employing scenarios, probabilities, and statistical analysis, in addition to extensive computer use and the building of risk-analysis models.

Chinese businesses use a "feel" technique rather than a sophisticated, quantifiable risk-analysis and management technique. Their costing is straight line and short term, and it seldom factors in intangible gains.

Be aware that this is another factor tending to boost your prices. The less certainty there is in costing and risk taking, the more the safety margin that will be built into prices.

The Market-Driven Economy

The American economy is market-driven and highly competitive. Our vast distribution system assures that consumers get the widest possible array of choices. Advertising, consumer mobility, freedom of competition, and shelf marketing are just a few of the many realities that affect marketing in America.

The Chinese are coming from an economic system that had, and still has, different characteristics. Consumers are not extremely mobile, distribution has limitations, income levels vary widely, utilitarian considerations outweigh style and convenience, and the consumer is not yet king (although some of these characterizations are now in the process of changing).

It is not surprising that Chinese manufacturers do not understand the market imperatives of the United States: the need for stringent quality testing, attractive packaging, and the most competitive pricing. On a recent trip, a Chinese manufacturer jokingly encapsulated our marketplace realities and the difficulties that the Chinese have with them.

He said "You Americans all want the same thing, the best quality *and* the lowest prices. Don't you realize that they work against each other?" We had to explain our market-driven economy's attributes and the necessity of trying to provide both of these two seemingly mutually exclusive goals.

The Negotiation Process

Successful negotiation requires that you know how to address all possible problems.

Some common American negotiating tactics teach us to maneuver to have the other guy make the first offer. Don't use that rule in China unless it's a brand-new product and you have no idea what the final result should be—and in that case you've come to the wrong country. The Chinese are masters of haggle-type negotiating.

Americans are usually goal-oriented and objective-oriented, while the Chinese often delight in the negotiation process itself, psychologically wearing you down. They wait until you think everything is wrapped up and finished, and then they spring requests that they have kept under wraps. Don't play the haggling game with them.

The first principle is this: Know everything you can about the products you intend to purchase or have made for you. How much is your toughest competitor selling the product for and what is the highest price that you can pay for it and still be able to compete successfully?

Don't negotiate prices unless you have solid knowledge of what you can and should pay for your products. You get the best prices by knowing your market and your competition. You must know what your products sell for and the best price anyone is paying for them and then dictate realistic, but better prices.

If the Chinese see that you really have all of that knowledge, and they are convinced that you are ready to buy now and only the price stands in the way, you stand a much better chance of getting the best price.

Americans tend to take a longer-term approach than do the Chinese, and have an understanding of loss leaders or a capacity to sustain possible losses on a first order, or willingness to invest in equipment that will be useful or necessary in getting more future orders. The Chinese do not take a product-lifetime approach to costing. They tend to want a guaranteed payback, over a shorter term.

Pitfalls to Avoid

Lack of cost accounting or thorough risk analysis techniques will result in getting quoted higher prices than you should pay. Furthermore, you don't want your potential partner to quote an artificially high price and then get locked into that higher price or lose face, therefore making the company reluctant to reduce the price in the future.

The better approach is to not ask them to quote before you have established the rules of the game. You'll win more games when you own the ball and set the rules.

The recommended rule here: Don't negotiate by haggling. Before negotiating, know the market and its pricing. Fix a maximum target price, above which you cannot buy and successfully sell the product. Be sure that in the specifications you include all testing and quality requirements as well as price, and make sure that pricing includes freight and duties to deliver the product where you want it. Then deduct 10 percent for margin of error, problems, and so on.

That is now the price that you must not go above. If your competition is already buying from China, be prepared to have to buy near your maximum target price. If your competition is not buying in China, deduct at least another 10 percent, minus freight, depending on the country of origin. If it's made in the United States, deduct at least 20 percent, minus all import charges. Then state to your source the price that it must make the product for.

Leave Room for Negotiation

There is one exception to the "no haggle" approach. The Chinese need to feel that their superior negotiating tactics have gained them advantages they would not have had otherwise. Therefore, when you draft your proposal, leave in it some points that you are prepared to concede so that they can change your proposal to their advantage by negotiating these preplanned points.

Estimate future sales if the quality and lead time is good. Ask your partner what its terms are. Common terms are 30 percent or 40 percent down on placing the order and 60 percent or 70 percent upon shipment; or 30 percent down upon placing the order, 30 percent upon sample approval and the start of production, and 40 percent upon shipment. Then, after some history, an open credit account should be established.

If you have succeeded in establishing very good rapport, you may be able to get a credit line established immediately.

When you give your Chinese counterparts the price that you are willing to pay, tell them how many units you will order on the first container. You must fill at least a small container (see Appendix 14 for container dimensions) and know how many units you will expect to fit into a container. A small container measures 20 feet; a large one is 40 feet.

If you have tailored your planned orders to fit a container, the Chinese company will know that you know international purchasing and are a serious buyer. This, in addition to removing all details that might cause your potential partner concern, paves the way for the company to offer the best prices possible.

It will also help if you explain the ramifications of the order. Stress the potential and the probability of future orders and their magnitude, and show your partner how you would cost it. Emphasize incremental and power costing. Explain how Americans use costing to break into new markets. Assure the company that you do not want it to lose money, and that you are willing to negotiate upward as well as downward if first orders go according to plan. There is no substitute for knowing your market and dictating low, realistic prices.

You will also need to take special steps to help your manufacturer understand clearly the necessity for top-notch quality control (QC) and packaging.

The Chinese have difficulty truly comprehending all the implications of quality control. They are used to thinking in terms of utility only. They are used to things breaking, and fixing them themselves. Up to now, this has been most people's economic experience. Looking for quality as well as price is a habit that is not yet well formed.

You may observe that manufacturers in China are not as proud of their product as they are of the trappings of wealth and power it brought.

Therefore, their appreciation of QC is something that you cannot take for granted. On QC, give potential partners very specific testing specifications: what exact tests need to be performed, under what exact conditions, and with what frequency. This requires a lot of detailed work on your part, but it must be done; if you leave any conditions to the imagination, shortcuts will be taken.

You may have to help your partner buy or build the proper testing equipment. You must be cautious about helping someone purchase anything. Require the party you are helping to sign an agreement stating that you do not assume any responsibility for anything you are purchasing, and that your purchasing the product does not in any way mitigate the other party's obligations to fulfill his negotiated responsibilities.

One American tried to help his Chinese partner by buying test equipment not available in China, and reselling it to his partner. Subsequently, a quality problem arose and the Chinese partner disclaimed responsibility because the American firm was the one who bought the test equipment.

Regarding packaging, the best course is to send a tangible example of the quality and type of packaging product that you are looking for. If you can't find exactly what you want, buy one closest to what you want. Your partner will appreciate more of the kind of quality packaging you need when he sees what's on the shelves now. Failing that, give very detailed specifications on the packaging alone. The peripheral industries are not as good on packaging in China as they are on some other services. If you need very special packaging, you may be forced to look elsewhere for it. Chinese manufacturers have made great progress in this area in the last couple of years, though, as foreign firms have come in.

Camouflaged Subjects to Negotiate

If you want to have products made that are not off-the-shelf, tooling costs will be an issue. Tooling up for your product can be an expensive proposition, but it's one that you will face no matter whom you work with, unless the manufacturer has made the exact same item for someone else, or has plans to sell it to others. Fortunately, tooling costs in China are much cheaper than they are here. Many manufacturers make their own tools. Check whether tooling can be avoided by buying from someone who has already made the tooling. If not, this is another item that must be negotiated. First, all things being equal, try to work with a firm that does its own tooling and feels comfortable doing it.

It is customary for the customer to pay the tooling charges and to own the tooling. The problem is that if you seek to change suppliers somewhere down the road, no matter what your contract says, you can't depend on a smooth transition. Unless you plan for this contingency, you will probably end up paying tooling charges again.

As in all contracts and agreements with the Chinese, anticipate why they will claim that they cannot perform as agreed. In the case of tooling, they may claim that the tooling has been rendered inoperative through use. Write into the contract that tooling must be made to withstand a minimum number of uses.

Depending on several factors, including the order quantity, complexity of tooling, your relationship with the manufacturer, and so on, your source may be willing to pay for, or at least participate in, the tooling costs.

In any case, tooling might become one of the factors by which you make your selection of vendors, and part of the whole package that you need to negotiate. Spell out in detail all of the tooling specifications—materials to be used, number of impressions guaranteed, and so on.

Another point that will enhance your negotiating position with your new source is to stress any new technology, information, and training that it will get. Both the government and the firm that you are negotiating with consider it a big plus to learn new technologies or to be trained in new processes and techniques. On the other hand, don't end up training a future competitor.

Agreements and Contracts

There are some differences in the way the Chinese view agreements that you must be aware of. Many people who have negotiated agreements with Chinese businessmen, only to have those agreements be a serious source of contention later, swear that the Chinese have no honor or honesty and can't be trusted. You should realize how the Chinese view agreements. In some countries, such as India, it may be more common for businessmen to set out to cheat you, plotting the method from the beginning. The Chinese, on the other hand, usually do not set out to cheat you, but you may feel that they end up treating you as though they did.

To most Americans, an agreement is our sacred word, to be lived up to until the agreement expires or until such time as both parties agree to change or cancel it. An agreement is our word, our honor, our bond, regardless of the legal implications. The Chinese, though, tend to view agreements completely differently. They view an agreement as a rough summary of intentions, and not binding if circumstances change.

Another factor is that the Chinese compartmentalize their agreements, contracts, and transactions. When they receive money, the money becomes theirs, and anyone who asks for some of it back to fix a problem or remedy a shortfall in performance becomes their adversary. Many have no sense of customer service or spending money to safeguard relationships. This is another instance where you can't count on the Chinese having the same attitudes and values that you have.

One agreement written according to these different points of view was between an American firm that wished to have a particular product it designed made in China, and a Chinese manufacturer that quoted an acceptable price to buy a guaranteed quantity at that price over the course of the next twelve months. On their second order, the invoice the American firm received was for substantially more than the agreed-upon price. The firm questioned the price, referring back to the agreement. "But the price of steel has risen 25 percent since then," complained the Chinese manufacturer. "You can't expect us to make your product at the same price." To no avail, the Americans argued that they had entered into agreements with customers to deliver at a fixed price, based on the contract price that had been agreed upon. "Then just tell them the circumstances and change the price," the manufacturer replied.

Most of the Chinese will not honor economic agreements (or political agreements, for that matter) if circumstances turn against them. In contrast, if you adhere to the agreement even if circumstances turn against you, but they do not, you are at a very distinct disadvantage.

When drafting the agreement, specifically state that prices are to remain the same, even if prices or costs to the manufacturer change. Try to think of all other circumstances that might prompt your partner to renege on the agreement and specifically include those also.

Put another way, American thinking is that the terms of a contract must be kept as long as the contract is in force or until both parties agree to change it. The Chinese believe that unless circumstances that may mitigate the benefits of the contract to them are agreed upon and made part of the contract, they are free to unilaterally change the terms if those negative circumstances occur.

Putting It in Writing

It is always a good idea to commit your understandings to writing. Don't leave areas that are later sources of misunderstanding. The Chinese do feel more committed to honor understandings when they are specifically agreed upon and expressed in writing, especially when a setback that would prompt them to go back on a promise is anticipated, and specific actions to take in that event have been agreed upon and addressed in the agreement.

Because the Chinese are not confrontational, they often leave certain difficult areas of agreement to work themselves out later, usually to the way they want it. Insist on getting all potentially conflicting areas resolved. Try to anticipate tough issues and problems, and come to agreement before starting your relationship. They will resist this, since they wish to avoid confrontation, but it's better to get agreement up front, or even to face non-agreement, than to have the gray areas sink you later.

Most of the Chinese do try to honor written agreements—private parties more so than government officials—especially if the issue that later causes the problem has been anticipated and addressed in the agreement.

Again, don't take for granted that your Chinese counterparts have the same assumptions you do. Be sure to address delivery problems, minimum quantities, quality issues, unmet specifications, cost increases, who pays for what, and all "what to do if . . ." issues.

Avoiding Cheats

Most Chinese people are honorable according to their own code, but just as in America or anywhere else, people differ. Some are not honorable, and set out to cheat. As stated elsewhere in this book, be sure that you know the reputation of the people you're dealing with. Cheats are known, since they have probably deceived other people before you, and while the Chinese are reluctant to say anything against friends or relatives, they will tell you about known cheats.

The best solution is to act to avoid problems rather than be injured and have to seek redress. Detail the breaches of ethics that can do you real damage. Then take practical steps to protect yourself.

First, follow a policy of giving out only the information that is absolutely necessary to conduct business. Then, if the information that you are giving out could hurt you if it fell into the wrong hands, leave out one or more key pieces, without which the information you give out cannot be useful to others.

For example, one American company makes a practice of having its engineers go over anything to be transmitted to a Chinese company. If it is giving out detailed plans to make a proprietary product, it does not give a complete product to any one company. The American company removes one or more key elements, without which the product being made cannot be completed. Sometimes, even the intended use of the product is unintelligible.

If the elements taken out of the specifications for the product are components that need to be made, they are given to a different company to make. Without the complete specifications for the whole product, the company making the missing key element hasn't any idea of its use or application either. The parts are sent separately to the U.S. firm by the companies who made them, and the product is assembled in America.

Legal Proceedings

Americans are trained to think in legal terms. Almost everyone in business in America is somewhat experienced with litigation. Not so in China.

A solid prediction is that Chinese litigation will burgeon in coming years, as news reports and word of mouth make litigation a more common alternative to private feuding, and the need grows to make agreements binding.

Although we dwelt earlier on the legal aspects of agreements (in Chapter 6), a key point is to not think in legal terms. A courtroom solution is definitely to be avoided. It is not a good option here in America, and it certainly isn't in China. As stated earlier, the most workable solutions are practical and embedded in a solid working relationship.

If you find yourself in a situation in which you have already been injured and you seek remedies, legal proceedings are becoming a viable option. American companies now are suing, and some are winning.

In the Corning case (described in Chapter 11), the decision was in Corning's favor. When the suit was brought, Corning was given little chance for success. The Chinese court decided that Corning in fact was not dumping and should not have been penalized. No fines were called for, and Corning was exonerated. Corning people see an even greater future in China.

This case may be a legal groundbreaker. An American company has prevailed in a Chinese court against the Chinese government on a very major issue. Other cases involving Americans that have recently been decided indicate that Americans are winning a good portion. This may signal a whole different legal environment for American firms.

Remember the pitfalls of legal process, especially in China. The laws are much more vague and open to interpretation. You should document in detail every alleged violation. Don't get into a situation in which it is your word against the other party's.

Other Negotiating Tips

The Chinese respect age and status. When it is time to negotiate, take an older associate with you, if practical. Title is very important. To get to top people in Chinese business or government, you need to be perceived as an important person, with title and power. People in China will pay attention to your title. "Chairman" is an important title. They equate it to "president."

Try to anticipate situations and problems, and get a clear definition of what will happen under those circumstances—who will have the responsibility and authority to do what. Be sure to cover all bases, including rate of exchange, future capital investment, terms, limits of the authority of the parties without notification—everything. Anticipation of problems and addressing potential problems before they happen promote continuing relationships.

Remember, you are the customer. The Chinese firm needs you at least as much as you need it, and probably more. You want a partner that's at least as flexible as you are.

After the Deal Is Made: Fostering Long-Term Relations

Don't let the Chinese people's quick acceptance of electronic gadgetry, and its prevalence, lead you to believe that the Chinese are sophisticated in everything.

Because they didn't get their business baptism by competitive fire, they are generally not as educated, experienced, or astute regarding modern business tools or the adroit application of specific information in making quick, incisive business decisions.

This book has pointed out the lack of modern accounting and risk-analysis techniques in China. There are many other instances of deficiencies in operating Chinese businesses.

Basically, the normal method of running businesses in China is much more subjective and can be compared to seat-of-the-pants management. Although the Chinese have embraced the computer for personal use and mundane work tasks, they don't know critical path or PERT (Program Evaluation and Review Techniques) or many other computer-aided management tools, nor do they use modern long-range planning methods. Long-range planning is not a formally recognized function at most Chinese companies.

If you want your employees or partners to use modern business techniques, you have some intense training ahead. After you have seen your partner's operation and understand how things are done now, you might point out to him how he could be more efficient and save money. It could improve your relationship and lead to lower costs. Be sure to make suggestions in a manner that does not attack his competence. Instead of criticizing his methods, perhaps you might tell him in general how things are done in the United States.

Setting Up Communications Links

Once you have an agreement put together, after much hard work, patience, attention to detail, and time, you can't just breathe a sigh of relief and leave it. A Chinese and American agreement is like a marriage. Not only does it take all kinds of time and effort to make the event happen; it takes constant attention afterward to keep it together.

You will have the obstacle of maintaining your relationship by using the impersonal tools of e-mail and fax, and the somewhat more personal telephone conversation, with perhaps only an occasional face-to-face contact.

To be successful, your relationship needs constant nurturing. Set up a communication schedule. Send e-mails about any issues in which your partner is involved. Ask for regular progress reports regarding work in progress, sent on predetermined forms by e-mail.

Call periodically. Set a time of day for scheduled calls, with a translator on your end. Get a number and time of day to call for unscheduled calls. If you will not have a translator available, then plan ways to communicate in emergencies. Perhaps the best timing is when your partner will have a translator.

Another alternative for verbal communication is to arrange for three-way calls with an off-premises translator with whom you contract. The benefits of having your own translator to help you make the deal have already been covered. That also goes for communicating after an agreement is reached.

If you are expecting to find a dearth of the latest technology, you will be surprised to learn that while there may be a lack of last-generation technology, there is seldom a lack of cutting-edge technology. The Chinese have embraced many appealing technologies even quicker than we have.

For instance, the Chinese have embraced wireless technology, while skipping the fax stage that we had. Few use faxes comfortably or well. Since faxes are seldom used, most fax machines are on dual-purpose lines.

Explain to them the role of faxes as well as other types of communications, and the possible need to dedicate a fax line 24/7, or at least during certain convenient hours for you. It is frustrating to be trying to fax something to your partner and constantly having someone who is not able to communicate with you answering the phone in voice mode.

Cell-phone usage in China far exceeds that of wired phones. Many Chinese have cell phones only, with no wired phones. However, many do not know how to place calls to America. Give them tips on calling, including dialing codes and best times to call (see "Time Zones" in Chapter 7 for more information about scheduling calls).

Every sophisticated Chinese business uses e-mail as an integral part of its communications. E-mail communications can be used instead of faxes. Most Chinese are more comfortable with e-mail because almost all businesses in China, even very small ones, use computers, and most have some way of connecting to the Internet.

The first thing to do is establish standards for communicating via computer. Make sure that you both have the same software for sending and reading drawings, graphics, and anything else you may use. This is another common problem with new relationships between an American firm and a

Chinese company. Don't assume that the Chinese have the same software or can read the formats that we are accustomed to.

Then, set a regular schedule of telephone calls to be preceded by e-mail agendas from all parties to the discussion, so that you can put together an agenda that will cover the topics they would like to discuss.

Praise

There is another point in furthering continued good personal relations that is counter to what we Americans are taught. We are taught to use a carrot-and-stick approach and to encourage positive behavior at least verbally. With many Chinese people, though, praise has an undesired effect.

If you praise the price, they think they could have gotten more. If you praise the quality, they think they don't have to be as careful. If you praise their timeliness, they feel they probably could have taken more time. Be sparing in your praise and be on the lookout for its possible negative effects.

Retaining and Extending Your Gains

If your agreement is one in which you have received permission to do something, lease something, or license something, you are even more apt to assume that the negotiating is ended when the promise is made or the agreement signed. As mentioned earlier, the Chinese do not consider agreements as necessarily permanent. In China, even a signed agreement requires regular maintenance.

Many American companies have discovered, to their chagrin, that a promise or even an agreement may not be honored if the relationship is not pursued. Relationships in which there is an underlying promise or agreement that continues to benefit you require diligent attention. Other competitors (especially Chinese ones) may want to usurp your benefits.

In the maintenance of these promises and agreements, be sure to cover all the bases. Anyone involved may be able to torpedo your agreement. This is especially true when you are dealing with the government. Be sure to establish and maintain relations with people at all levels who might have a say in the agreements. Keep everyone on your side and stay informed on current events. Avoid unpleasant surprises.

After the excitement and novelty of going to China have worn off, the key people who put the agreement together in the first place tend not to return very often. There is no substitute for personal visits (accompanied by gifts). It shows intense interest like nothing else can.

If you set up permanent operations in China, frequent personal visits and/or long-term stays are a must. This is especially important if you make a high-level personnel change. If someone who contacted customers, suppliers, or government personnel leaves or is terminated, it is imperative for you to make immediate personal visits to all who had come in contact with him to show continuity and continued support.

Once you have set up an operation in China and have hired your key people, you have established momentum, an excitement, a climate of expectation on the part of your people, your customers, the people who helped you in the establishment process (including government people), and even your competitors.

If there is little perceived forward progress immediately after establishment, you lose that momentum and a valuable advantage.

Plan to take immediate advantage of the climate your business created by training your people quickly, gaining ISO status quickly, and showing off your new facility to all your customers and new friends and acquaintances. Most of all, mount a strong sales effort as soon as practical and make sure before you depart that the momentum and forward movement will continue. Let everyone know that your company is there to stay and that you mean business.

Business Opportunities in China by Industry

Much of our discussion has been for general, nonspecific information and use. Part Four sets forth some of the specific business opportunities that are available in China.

Chapter 14 lists key industries individually and the current prospects for each, organized by nonagricultural goods and services and then by agricultural goods and services. Much of this information is culled from official U.S. government assessments and may be more pertinent to those people already engaged in those specific industries.

Chapter 15 is much more subjective and stems from personal observations and evaluations. It is more intuitive than statistical and may be of more interest to entrepreneurs interested in setting up new businesses or expanding into China.

Chapter 14

Export Opportunity Industries

THE FOLLOWING SECTIONS describe your best prospects for business opportunities in China, first in nonagricultural goods and services, and then in the agricultural sector.

Telecommunications Equipment

China's WTO accession will eventually lead to an opening of the market for value-added services. Under the WTO, China has made commitments in three areas:

1. Key telecommunications services in the Beijing, Shanghai, and Guangzhou areas, which carry more than two-thirds of all domestic traffic, are open to foreign competition. Foreign carriers will be permitted up to 25 percent ownership in mobile services and 30 percent ownership in value-added services.
2. All geographic restrictions for value-added services is being be phased out. Geographic restrictions on mobile services and on domestic wireless services will be phased out within a few years.
3. Forty-nine percent foreign ownership will be permitted in mobile services shortly in seventeen major cities, and within a few years for all of China. Forty-nine percent ownership will be permitted for international and domestic fixed-line services and 50 percent for value-added services.

The best sub-sector prospects within this sector include mobile and value-added capabilities for e-mail and Web browsers and the ability to download ringtones, logos/images, music, videos, games, stock-market quotations, and so on.

With the changes agreed to for the mobile market under the WTO, U.S. carriers and value-added providers should have good opportunities in the Chinese telecommunications market in the future.

Oil and Gas

China's overall energy consumption ranks second in the world. China's growing demand has caused this traditionally off-limits sector to gradually open up to increasingly larger-scale foreign participation. Reluctance to change has made progress in the oil and gas sector slow for foreign firms in China, but government encouragement has produced progress.

The best opportunities for foreign participation are in natural gas infrastructure development and offshore oil exploration and production. Onshore oil projects are far less attractive due to lack of access to satisfactory leverage and geological data and a greater tendency to source equipment, services, and technology domestically. Offshoot industries with high-technology components are in high demand.

Medical Equipment

China's medical device market is the largest in Asia outside of Japan, and one of the fastest-growing in the world. American firms provide more than a third of total imported products in this category, followed by Japan and Germany.

U.S. products are viewed by Chinese end users as being of superior quality and possessing the highest level of advanced technology. The domestic industry is consolidating, upgrading, and beginning to compete on medium-level technologies.

Most of the Chinese, as many as 80 percent, lack health insurance, and only 5 percent of the population can afford top-end Western medical care. The ongoing reforms are not designed to expand the number of insured, but rather to replace government funding with enterprise/employee funding. In the past, all government employees and workers at state-owned enterprises enjoyed virtually free medical care for themselves and their dependents. A new urban medical insurance system was introduced in 2000, with the goal of offering basic health care to urban workers. More than 80 million urbanites are covered under this system so far.

Pharmaceuticals

China is one of the largest pharmaceutical markets in the world, with nearly $10 billion in sales. China's changing health-care environment is designed to extend basic health insurance to a larger portion of the population and give individuals greater access to products and services.

The dietary supplements sub-sector is huge and growing very rapidly.

High-quality foreign-made products account for only a bit over 10 percent of total sales. Companies report that complicated product registration, expensive and time-consuming certification requirements, and inexperienced and inefficient distributors are common obstacles in China.

However, the government is starting to address these problems, and dynamic growth is expected.

As foreign pharmaceutical firms gain a measure of control over their distribution and are able to re-educate health professionals in the use of orally administered, more effective Western medications as an alternative to intravenous delivery of less-effective products, hospitals will find that they save time, space, and money. Major growth opportunities should then present themselves.

Pollution-Control Equipment

Spending on environmental protection during the tenth Five-Year Plan period (2001–2005) is projected to have reached 1.4 percent of GDP. The Chinese government is seriously trying to ease the pollution situation, preserve the environment, and improve environmental quality in key cities and regions, as well as expand environmental-protection policies, laws, and regulations.

There have been some successes in this governmental effort to gain control over pollution, but the economic growth during the 2001–2005 period has been so dynamic that in fact, the environment is in worse shape than it was five years ago.

It is clear that much more money and effort are needed in the next five years to make significant progress on this front. The prediction is that if China does not increase its efforts in the environmental area, pollution levels will triple by 2015, which will make many places unlivable. The largest factors in these predictions are increased electricity production using mostly coal, the expected explosion of private car ownership, and the economic boom that is creating the huge industrial expansion.

The overall pollution-control equipment market is growing rapidly, but only a portion of it is practically accessible to foreign firms due to financing and hard currency constraints, low-cost local competition, closed bidding practices, and other market barriers. The government seems to have a sincere desire to make real progress on the environmental front, though, including easing practical restrictions on foreign competition. It is reasonable to expect much easier entry into the field in the very near future.

Most large U.S. environmental firms have concentrated on World Bank and Asian Development Bank projects. The future will be even brighter as affluent key cities in China begin to dramatically increase environmental spending, multinational investors uncover sources of demand, and municipalities experiment with new project financing models.

There are several factors that will propel China's environmental market to become one of the world's largest. The fact that governmental and personal income levels will continue to rise in a huge country with acute environmental needs already is one basic factor.

However, other factors are also at work. China has long been secretive, especially about mistakes and bad news. This is equally true of the reporting procedures for environmental news. Disasters are routinely not reported. Recently, though, the public has realized this tendency and has been vocal about it. The people are voicing a right to know about environmental disasters, which is putting more pressure on governments to more accurately portray dangers. The Central Government is now forcing local governments to be more forthcoming. This will undoubtedly also increase pressure for more environmental control equipment in the future.

However, American companies may find that competitors from other developed countries have already gained firm beachheads, because these firms are now winning contracts with the help of subsidized loans, grants, and other tied aid from their governments. There is a strong case for the U.S. government to become proactive.

Insurance Industry

The insurance industry has shown rapid growth within the past few years, particularly the life insurance market, as average annual incomes have grown. In addition, the increasing number of private businesses, coupled with the decline of job opportunities in the state sector as a result of China's state reforms, has sparked people's interest in buying all types of insurance, ranging from property to life. This trend should continue strongly, making for great opportunities in this sector.

According to the China Insurance Regulatory Commission (CIRC), China's insurance industry should maintain annual growth rate of 12 percent. Other experts forecast greater market growth, up to about $120 billion by the end of this decade.

Growth of the insurance sector is poised to continue with effective implementation of China's WTO commitments.

Market access barriers such as restrictive licensing have been addressed. China has agreed to grant licenses on a prudential basis, without numerical restrictions or discretionary "economic needs" tests. Companies can obtain a license if they have more than thirty years of experience in a WTO member country, a representative office established in China for two consecutive years; and global assets of more than $5 billion.

Insurance certainly represents one of the best future opportunities for American business.

Airport and Ground-Support Equipment

During the five years ending 2005, China added more than 300 planes to its airlines; accelerated airport construction; updated the technical grade of the major airports; enhanced air passenger/cargo handling capacity; added advanced air traffic radar and telecommunication and navigation facilities; built and improved flight systems; established a national, centralized, and unified air traffic control system; strengthened the construction of aircraft maintenance bases; and developed regional aviation. Priority is given to airports constructed in the western region.

China has more than 170 civil airports including 3 large national hub airports, 6 medium-sized hub airports, and more than 160 trunk line and regional airports.

Airport development and construction covers a wide range of products and services, including initial design and engineering services; construction equipment; specialized runway and air traffic control equipment; airport security systems and equipment; cargo inventory management facilities; telecommunications; x-ray equipment; scales; emergency vehicles; and even retail concessions and airport management services.

Specialized training for air traffic controllers could also be grouped under this broad and growing sector of the aviation market.

With a country geographically as large as China, and with tourism revenues growing rapidly, air cargo volume rapidly increasing, and the general population enjoying more and more discretionary income for travel, the government has placed a high priority on improving the entire air travel system and in fact, it is being done.

China's future aviation market promises to be spectacular. Since the Chinese see U.S. companies as the world leaders in many of these aviation categories, American companies have exceptional opportunity here.

Building/Decorations Materials

Among the hottest market sectors in China is the home building/decorations materials industry. Liberalization of ownership restrictions by the government coupled with rapid growth in housing construction makes this market increasingly attractive. Of the two, the home decorations market is experiencing the more rapid growth, which is expected to continue development at a growth rate of 25 percent to 30 percent annually.

Augmenting this sustained growth are the following sub-sector categories:

1. Acrylic and vinyl-based paints
2. Granite crude/rough
3. Coniferous wood veneer sheets
4. Doors, windows, frames, and thresholds
5. Aluminum doors, windows, and frames
6. Plasters
7. Sinks, wash basins, and stainless steel products
8. Sanitary fixtures, porcelain/china
9. Other miscellaneous structural materials

The Chinese government recently reported that the annual growth rate for housing is already between 20 percent and 25 percent.

Automotive Parts

China is making efforts to develop its automotive industry into a pillar industry in the national economy by 2010.

China's accession to the WTO is having a great impact on the automotive industry. By the end of 2006, tariffs on imported automobiles will be reduced to 25 percent. Tariffs on imported automotive parts in 2006 will reduce components' tariffs to 10 percent. The gradual reduction of tariffs on automotive parts and China's agreement to eliminate local content requirements will place domestic automotive parts manufacturers in direct competition with their international counterparts on an almost level field.

Compared to international companies, few leading Chinese auto parts firms spend much on research and development (R & D). In the next five years, the Chinese government will continue to encourage foreign investment in automotive component development and manufacturing.

There is definitely a growing market for imports, and American products are generally highly regarded among Chinese customers.

Domestic OEM firms encourage U.S. suppliers to establish plants in China or work more closely with Chinese firms to upgrade product quality.

Agricultural Chemicals

China's agriculture-related market has been the subject of great attention. Agrochemical exports to China are very important for U.S. industries. China ranks as the top destination among U.S. fertilizer exports in recent years, and that opportunity is expected to continue.

Plastic Materials and Resins

China's output of plastic materials and resins can only satisfy 50 percent of market demand. As a result, it must import large quantities of plastic materials each year. The local market requires imports of general-purpose thermoplastic resins, including polyethylene (LDPE and HDPE), polypropylene (PP), polystyrene (PS), acrylonitrile butadiene styrene (ABS), and polyvinyl chloride (PVC).

China needs to import large amounts of synthetic resins to meet local market demand.

Special engineering plastics and other resins, which possess special physical and chemical properties, are used widely in various industries as special materials. U.S.-engineered plastic products have high-technology inputs and are very competitive in the Chinese market. However, U.S. firms now face stiff competition from Japan, Korea, Taiwan, and Germany. In recent years, imports of general plastics from the United States dropped sharply due to price competition and the close relationship between some Asian competitors and China, but with more attention to relationships and with a stronger marketing effort, U.S. firms should reverse this recent downturn.

Food-Packaging Equipment

Under China's economic reform policies, most industries, including the food, printing, plastics, pharmaceutical, and chemical industries, have developed rapidly. There are many recently instituted regulations on food packaging. This has resulted in increasing demand for packaging, and therefore packaging machinery.

There is increasing demand in the Chinese market for high-quality packaging. This provides excellent opportunities for American packaging-equipment firms. The Chinese are starting to realize that better packaging capabilities means more export possibilities.

China tends to source less-sophisticated equipment from domestic sources to save money. However, Chinese customers are interested in importing complex, high-performance machinery that has no domestically manufactured equivalent. Price is always a prime consideration. Some companies claim that they are willing to pay a five- to ten-fold premium for American manufactured products and that they anticipate buying more when possible in order to improve the overall quality of the end product and to meet new rules and regulations.

Packaging firms value foreign-made machinery for its fast packaging speed, automation, quality, and reliability. A common sentiment is that Chinese-made machinery is adequate for some applications but that foreign-made machinery can be more profitable for complex packaging needs or lines that require continuous operation. Other major considerations are the reduced requirement for manpower and maintenance realized by using imported machinery.

In China, packaging usage continues to grow at around 20 percent annually, and the importation of food-packaging equipment continues to rise as well. The best sub-sector prospects within this sector include the following:

- Filling/closing machinery (including bottling or can-sealing machines), which constitutes about 50 percent of the total packaging-equipment market
- Packing/wrapping machinery, which constitutes about 30 percent of the total packaging-equipment market
- Parts, with a market share of about 15 percent

Additionally, China is increasingly using honeycomb paperboard packaging instead of wooden crates, which also provides opportunities for American manufacturers of honeycomb paperboard packaging equipment.

Export Opportunity Industries: Agricultural

In this section, we'll run through the best prospects in China for agricultural and animal goods and services.

Grains: Wheat, Corn, and Barley

The best prospects are for feed grains. Other near-term prospects are not as good.

Grass Seed

China is in the process of beautifying cities, improving its animal forage industry, and combating desert expansion and soil erosion. China will likely import greater amounts of grass seed as it returns more farmland to grassland and forest. This market is extremely price-sensitive, though, and China tends to buy cheaper forage seed instead of higher-priced varieties. If a much better case for the benefits of higher-priced varieties could be put together, and put before the right people, it could have a great impact on buying habits.

Oilseeds: Soybeans, Soybean Meal, and Soybean Oil

Long-term prospects for soybeans and soybean products remain extremely promising. As incomes rise and diets improve, demand for both vegetable oil and soymeal for livestock feed has boomed.

Poultry Meat

Poultry meat is a large and growing import market. The market, though, is a very singular one. China produces enough chicken muscle meat to satisfy the domestic market and even to export to Japan and Korea. However, Chinese cuisine creates a strong demand for chicken offal as well. Because this offal sells for low prices in the United States and other countries where local tastes produce only a slight demand, exports to China are very attractive. The United States dominates the import market.

Hides and Skins

China is a major market for imported bovine hides and skins, which are processed and used to manufacture finished leather goods for both the domestic and export markets. U.S. hides are extremely competitive because the finished leather export industry relies on high-quality hides for raw materials. In addition, the demand for U.S. hides should grow as foreign-invested tanneries relocate to China for cost reasons.

Snack Foods

Improved living standards, combined with developing distribution/retail systems, will continue to generate consistent demand for high-quality U.S. snack foods and other products that do not directly compete with Chinese domestic production.

Fresh Fruits

Although China's fruit production is large, important U.S. export opportunities still exist because of the country's poor post-harvest storage, handling practices, and facilities. There is particular need for fresh fruit during the Chinese New Year Festival and in cities with an improving standard of living.

A large amount of China's fresh-fruit imports enter the country through Guangdong province, which borders Hong Kong. From Guangdong, the fruit is then distributed to most of China's major cities. In time this will change, as distribution improves and becomes more competitive and as government regulations change.

Beef and Pork

Growth in beef imports continues. About half of all beef imports are beef offal. The most popular cuts of imported beef offal are stomach and tendons. The pork import market, although very large, is exclusively offal.

With limited land resources constraining beef production, and incomes continuing to rise, long-term prospects for medium to high-quality beef cuts are also good.

Dairy Ingredients

China's demand for dairy products has increased greatly over the last several years. Demand has grown the most for fluid milk, including yogurt and flavored dairy drinks. The U.S. shares of fluid milk and powdered milk markets have increased greatly.

Even with the strong consumption growth, China's per capita milk consumption is approximately only 8.79 (or 19.3 pounds) kg per year, among the lowest in the world. For the long term, as incomes rise and consumers continue to develop a taste for dairy products, the outlook and potential for large increases in dairy-product sales are excellent.

This is another market in which strong advertising would pay very large long-term dividends. Cooperative advertising to gain consumer favor for the product would be more important initially than would brand advertising.

Seafood

Lower-priced salmon, such as chum and pink salmon, is much appreciated in China. Alaskan crab is well liked in China and is considered a delicacy by hotels and consumers.

Forest Products

Forest product imports continue to grow rapidly, and prospects for continued growth are excellent. Consumption is growing at the same time domestic supplies are declining due to continued efforts to preserve natural forests and improve harvesting practices. These factors drive increased import demand.

The government's housing-reform campaign has helped stimulate consumption by increasing the demand for wood products used for interior decoration and furniture. Demand for hardwood products is great in fancy plywood production and interior decoration uses. There has also been considerable growth in the construction of wood-frame housing. The size of this market is limited by building codes that do not recognize Western-style wood-frame construction, but these codes may change soon.

Chapter 15

Fast-Growing Opportunities in China

NOW THAT CONSUMERISM has taken hold in China and is destined to grow strongly, the number of economic opportunities existing there is great. Although this book takes up the more apparent ones, if you looked for opportunity in your own field specifically, you would probably be rewarded by seeing individualized opportunity.

This country is becoming a petri-dish environment of opportunity, with government incentive plans, fast-growing incomes and areas, and fast-changing tastes, combined with a population willing to embrace all manner of changes, from Western culture to fashion, technology, and family values. Rapidly evolving environments present all manner of opportunity for the creative mind.

Growth and opportunities are always uneven. You might look at the industries that have not been a part of the Chinese way of life in the past, as well as supporting industries in areas where a major industry has developed but the industries needed to support that major industry are lagging.

The latter are specialized and too numerous to mention, but here is a look at some favorites in the first category.

Insurance and Financial Services

We took insurance earlier, but I bring it up again because it is so large and replete with opportunities for aggressive American companies.

Insurance is becoming a major growth industry in China because more and more of the Chinese are becoming aware of it, and its objectives fit the Chinese inclination to protect what they have. Many American companies are entering the fray, and many who are there already are expanding rapidly. There is major opportunity in this area.

As more people enter the middle class and begin to accumulate some savings, there is also a great opportunity for financial services. Most Chinese people trust Americans, which adds to the opportunity.

Education

The whole field of education is brimming with exciting opportunities in China. Almost all of the urban Chinese want their children to get a good education. They admire American education techniques, and as a result, so-called American-style schools are popular, even though many do not offer American-style education at all. Chinese education methods are very different, stressing rote memory instead of concepts. American schools, American educational materials, and other American services or products would probably be quite successful. This opportunity extends to educational toys, games, and books.

Also, the Chinese recognize that quality English-language education will be very beneficial for their children, and they will pay a premium to be taught by Americans.

Health and Medical

The Chinese do not keep complete and accurate statistics on many things, especially problems such as health, but it is clear with just empirical evidence that not only are more visitors to China getting sick there, but also more native Chinese are getting sick for longer periods than at any time in the recent past, and the rate of illnesses is growing.

A much higher percentage of the people than was previously the case are sick at any given time or have just gotten over being sick. Of course, you need to keep in mind that these observations were made in urban centers. Increased illness is probably due to several factors, including fast-increasing populations, urban conditions, increased mobility of the population, air quality, laxity of enforcement of food preparation and handling regulations, and personal and cultural hygienic standards.

There is a rapidly growing interest in fitness and leisure-time sports among urban professionals. This blossoming interest can be attributed mainly to the growing incomes and emulation of American culture.

Some Western companies, such as Bally and W. L. Gore (Gore-Tex waterproof fabric) have put resources toward promoting this trend. Bally has a number of fitness clubs in major coastal cities and plans to expand to about 100 clubs in coming years.

With the rise in disposable income, private clinics and the demand for health checkups are growing rapidly. Since Americans are seen as leading the advances in drugs and medicines, there are opportunities for American firms in this field, also.

Many Chinese believe that American medical technology and drugs are the best in the world, which offers us expanded medical and health opportunities. The field is heavily regulated, but for companies with money, patience, and expert advisers, there are many outstanding opportunities.

Entertainment

With more income and more leisure time comes an increasing propensity to enjoy different forms of entertainment.

Movies, plays, musicals, and theme parks were mentioned earlier. While the core entertainment is American, the procedures used to successfully introduce them into China are different from what they are in the United States, and some adaptations may be needed.

The financial arrangements of staging musicals in China differ from those in the United States. Here, almost all costs are paid by private investors for a share of profits, whereas in China the producer usually sells the rights to a Chinese partner for a fee. Sometimes the producer will also take a share of the gate.

Chinese theaters sometimes get funding from corporate sponsors for perhaps 30 percent of the expenses. Amway's cosmetic brand "Artistry" was the top sponsor for a production of *The Phantom of the Opera* in Shanghai.

Sometimes script changes are needed to help audiences understand what's going on because of the differences in culture and customs.

Financial arrangements for musicals, not unlike arrangements in other business areas, are laced with unexpected problems. Some potential partners do not have the wherewithal to carry out their part of the bargain, and they simply vanish.

Sports events are a neglected area that should be probed. There are many upscale, urban Chinese consumers who are fascinated with finding new forms of entertainment. They now regularly watch Houston Rockets basketball games to see Yao Ming play. Some baseball games are available for viewing. By first gaining fans with television offerings, a Chinese market could be created for Western-style sports events, perhaps eventually followed by professional sports leagues.

Hong Kong Disneyland, as mentioned in Chapter 4, is a giant experiment in transporting entertainment. Another entertainment area that could blossom is live concerts featuring American musical performers.

One obstacle to staging events for the Chinese public is that it may require "seeding." That is, exposing the Chinese to events at no charge in order to pique their interest and attempt to capture their loyalty and build their desire to see other similar events, thus guiding them to a point at which they become fans willing to pay for events that they enjoy. This may require a great deal of effort and creativity, but the payoff could be fantastic for those with foresight.

An example of latent power to influence and make money that has accrued to Americans is exemplified by the phenomenal success of a book about the life of the former Chinese leader Jiang Zemin. A Chinese publisher, Shanghai Century Publishing Group, has printed one million copies of a book by Lawrence Kuhn, an American, that was titled *The Man Who Changed China: The Life and Legacy of Jiang Zemin*. Mr. Kuhn does not speak or read Chinese, and about 10 percent of the book was censored.

It not only points out the strong curiosity that many Chinese have about the secretive people who have run their country, but also the respect that professional Americans have for research and presentation of facts and events.

Environmental Protection and Waste Disposal

Environmental and waste concerns is another area in which American technology and experience affords people who possess the knowledge and experience some strong opportunities. This is an area where you really need some competent advice from people familiar with the appropriate government officials. The government is paying more attention to the environment and is trying to establish the right policies. Americans who can capture the ear of the right people in China will succeed in this area in a major way.

Franchising

China is just now in the process of passing laws and regulations that specifically address franchising. Many foreign companies have established multiple retail outlets under a variety of creative arrangements, including some that, for all practical purposes, function like franchises.

Virtually all of the foreign companies that operate multiple-outlet retail venues in China either manage the retail operations themselves with Chinese partners (typically establishing a different partner in each major city) or sell to a master franchisee, which then leases out and oversees several franchise territories within the territory.

Restrictions on equity share, number of outlets, and geographical area are soon to be eliminated. The State Economic and Trade Commission is currently drafting new franchising laws.

China is now allowing more liberalized rules in recruiting and vetting (screening) of prospective franchisees and more attention to the protection of brand and property rights. These new franchise rules allow more direct franchising and make it more attractive to prospective franchisees. Previously, there was a real fear that companies could lose control of their trade secrets and brands. The best way to "franchise" was to set up offshore entities.

The changing image of how business is viewed has helped the franchise business as well as business in general. Businessmen used to be poorly regarded in traditional China, but are now admired, and entrepreneurship is now highly accepted. This has swelled the ranks of prospective franchisees.

Already, many American franchisors are very successful. Starbucks now has more than 200 locations in Mainland China. McDonald's, which opened in China in the early 1990s, has 600 locations, and they are—and have been— very profitable. In September 2004, McDonald's received government permission to formally franchise.

Many more permissions have now been granted, obviating the necessity to go through organizational gymnastics to achieve the franchise objective.

Pizza Hut and KFC (owned by Yum! Brands, Inc.) are two other success stories that required some changes from their normal American pattern. Pizza Hut has had great success with salad bars that allow only one trip. This has become something of a contest with the Chinese, who spend much time and imagination building salad bowls that are taller than any I have seen here. The pizza itself has also caught on with some differences in toppings and a studied approach to which flavorings appeal here. Most Pizza Hut franchises have waiting lines to be seated at popular mealtimes.

KFC, which has been in China since 1987, has also been successful with changes to its American menu. Most of the Chinese have no idea of the company's chicken-based history. In China it is viewed as another McDonald's-type outlet. KFC franchises now total more than 1,200.

Franchising, not only for food outlets, but also for other things that are popular in the United States, such as retail electronics, convenience stores, specialized business services, and so on, holds great potential opportunity for Americans, since many Chinese want to emulate the American lifestyle.

Also, the Chinese will almost certainly emulate certain buying habits and preferences of the Western world, such as brand names and stores that seem larger and more reliable and have name recognition. Franchising affords an opportunity to build a company with many outlets, and to avail yourself of the image and advantages of a large company without the same direct investment required of a company-owned store chain.

Convenience Products

One way to tell what a country has unfulfilled demand for is to see what frequent travelers to other countries bring back with them. Chinese airline pilots, for example, take back with them cases of Huggies diapers and other convenience items. What does that tell us?

Chinese buying habits have generally been strictly utilitarian. People in China bought products that were cheap and performed the function that they were supposed to perform. The Chinese didn't have the option of choosing products that were easier to use, more convenient, safer, disposable, and so on. Their buying habits were tempered by the amount of their disposable incomes and the availability of competing products. With disposable income rising, middle-class Chinese consumers are now willing to pay for products that offer time savings and convenience. China is a market that is ready for convenience products.

Luxury Goods

In terms of luxury and image products, the Chinese are becoming more Westernized. When they are making the grade, they want other people to know it. Many luxury stores, such as fine jewelry stores and women's couturier shops, are already doing well.

It is estimated that more than 13 percent of the population of China can afford to purchase luxury-class goods. That number is expected to rise more than 20 percent per year for the next few years, creating a huge latent demand for luxury and image-branded products, despite the counterfeiting problem. Knowledgeable Chinese consumers are learning how to tell a counterfeit product from the real thing, and they want people to know that they can afford the real thing.

This is another area in which educating people could develop their taste for your goods and a demand that would never be there without an education or exposure process first. There will be much more conspicuous consumption in China. The more that people can distinguish different standards of quality, the bigger the market for quality you create.

Conclusion

China:
Opportunities Await

THERE ARE MANY OPPORTUNITIES to make money in China today, and many more chances to lose money. Make sure that you're not rowing against the tide. If the government doesn't want your type of business, you will have an uphill fight. As it is here, many more people will lose money than make it, but the opportunities are great for those with imagination.

Americans are the premier entrepreneurs—seasoned competitors. We are more exposed to and more experienced in business, especially retailing and services, than our Chinese counterparts; we are more advanced and better trained in the use of cutting-edge business techniques as well as gathering, analyzing, and using information and statistics.

If you have a special product, skill, or service that you believe is needed in China, seriously consider doing business there. While the Chinese know their culture better than we do, of course, we can better predict where the next trends will lead them, since, to a large extent in recent years, their tastes and buying patterns have more closely mirrored ours.

The Chinese are anxious to improve their quality of life and their standard of living, and to share in the world's prosperity. If you have the technology, knowledge, and experience that will improve or impact some aspect of life there, and you have the understanding, patience, and resources to overcome disappointments along the way, now is the time to tell your story and establish your business in China.

APPENDIXES

| **Shopping**

If you are planning to spend some personal time shopping in China, you should patronize only the legitimate shopping districts. In most major cities, there also is a black-market shopping district, full of bootleg and counterfeit merchandise, such as "$25 Rolex watches." As support of this industry should not be encouraged, none of these districts are listed here. Pricing in such districts is always heavily dependent on negotiation, and quality is not at all uniform.

Most prices in legitimate districts are set and there is little negotiation. However, since labor costs are so much cheaper, and shopping where the goods are produced cuts out one or two middleman markups, you should find some good values for goods made in China, as compared to prices in the United States.

In order to get close to the best prices possible, you need to know the normal cost of the items you're looking for and then see if you can negotiate down from there depending on nearby competition. (See Chapter 13 for more about negotiation.) You also should know what constitutes quality in the products you are seeking.

The following describes some of the best shopping districts in major Chinese cities:

Shanghai *Nanjing Street* is three and a half miles of shopping fun. One of the largest shopping districts anywhere, it is now a pedestrian zone with more than 600 stores and shops.

Appendix 1 | Shopping

Beijing *Wangfujing Street* has all kinds of goods, including famous brands, in a wide variety of shops. *Old-Beijing-Street* is a large underground shopping area featuring well-known and long-established stores selling various merchandise, food stuffs, and authentic Chinese items and designs.

Xian *Huajue Xiang* is a narrow shopping lane filled with vendors of antiques, souvenirs, arts and crafts, and other miscellaneous items. Be prepared to bargain for everything. Be very careful, as quality varies widely, but prices should be less than in the larger cities. Another shopping opportunity is outside the East Gate by the Baxian Temple every Wednesday and Sunday, where villagers bring in various antique goods. Depending upon your expertise in judging antique values, this can be an exciting and rewarding shopping experience.

Shenyan *Zhong Street* and *Taiyuan Jie* are the two largest commercial areas and are known as providing the best shopping in northeastern China. The city is known for feather paintings, silk flowers, mosaics, and jade carvings.

Guangzhou *Beijing Road* has now grown to rival some of Hong Kong's shopping attractions, and at significantly lower prices. Most shops are open 10 A.M. to 10 P.M. The area now features international name-brand boutiques and branches of Hong Kong department stores.

Shen Zhen *Dong Men Shopping District* is an open-air shopping area with more than a hundred shops. This is a "bargaining" district, where you should get more than 50 percent off regular prices. Many counterfeits are sold here and the quality of regular goods varies, so it's definitely "buyer beware."

Hong Kong   *Tsim Sha Tsui (TST)*, at the tip of Kowloon Peninsula, is the largest and most famous shopping district in this famous shopping city. *Peking Road* has a plethora of jewelers. *Nathan Road*, known as "The Golden Mile" is a unique shopping experience

Tian Jin   *Binjiangdao* and *Hepinglu Commercial Streets* intersect each other, and they are the busiest areas with the most famous shopping entities; night shopping there is an interesting experience. Locals can direct you to several other shopping areas in the city.

Chengdu   *Heping District* is the main shopping are. The city is famous for various silk fabrics, varieties of lacquer ware, and bamboo works on porcelain.

If you are in a city not listed here, ask the concierge at your hotel about shopping areas.

Almost every large city now has a major shopping district accessible by public transportation. Most people don't have a private car, so shopping centers located away from the transportation systems are not yet in evidence, but they will probably start popping up in the next several years.

China ran a $100 billion trade surplus in 2005. This is triple the 2004 surplus, and it is expected to further increase in 2006.

Economic growth has topped 9 percent for the third year in a row.

Net exports are more than half of economic growth.

FDI (Foreign Direct Investment) dropped in 2005.

China's GDP is 4 percent of the global total, but consumption of energy sources is 12 percent and water consumption is 15 percent.

United States exports to China have been rising by about 15 percent a year.

Consumer prices in China rose less than 2 percent in 2005.

Retail growth is rising faster than GNP and exceeded 12 percent in 2005.

There are currently more than 280,000 foreign-invested companies in China.

Retail sales of consumer goods are now over RMB 5 trillion ($625 billion USD).

United States exports to China were up 80 percent from 2001 to 2005.

There are 4,000 skyscrapers in Shanghai—twice as many as in New York City.

About 300 million people (23 percent) in China are considered middle class.

Pronouns

English	Pinyin	Pronunciation
I, me	wo	*woh*
we, us	women	*wohmen*
you (singular)	ni	*nee*
you (plural)	nimen	*neemen*
he, she, it	ta	*tah*
they, them	tamen	*tahmen*

Expressions and Words

English	Pinyin	Pronunciation
Greeting (How are you?)	ni hou	*nee how*
Goodbye	zai jian	*zye zheean*
Thank you	xie xie	*see-eh see-eh*
You're welcome (It's okay)	bu ke qi	*boo keh tsee*
Sorry	dui bu qi	*dway boo tsee*
My name is . . .	wo shi . . .	*woh sheh . . .*
What is your name?	ni jiao shenme	*nee gee-ah-oh shen-meh*
Where is . . .	zai nar li . . .	*zie nar lee . . .*
Factory	gong chang	*gohn chahn*
Bathroom	ce suo	*tzeh soo-oh*
Right! (agreeing)	dui	*dway*
How much does this cost?	Duo shao qian	*duoh shah-oh tseeahn*
We appreciate your hospitality	xie xie ni de kuan dai	*see-eh see-eh nee deh kuahn dye*
Good	hou	*how*
Bad	bu hou	*boo how*

| # Chinese Words and Phrases

Numbers

English	Pinyin	Pronunciation	Tone
0	ling	*ling*	(flat tone)
1	yi	*yee*	(flat tone)
2	er	*ar*	(down tone)
3	san	*sahn*	(flat tone)
4	si	*sir*	(down tone)
5	wu	*woo*	(down tone, then up)
6	liu	*leeo*	(down tone)
7	qi	*tsee*	(flat tone)
8	ba	*bah*	(flat tone)
9	jiu	*jee-o*	(down tone, then up)
10	shi	*sheh*	(up)

| # How to Use Chopsticks

1. Rest the end of the lower chopstick in the V between your thumb and forefinger. Support the chopstick with the side of the ring finger.
2. Hold the upper chopstick between your middle finger and index finger, and anchored with your thumb, as if it were a pencil.
3. Make sure the tips of the chopsticks are always even, and the same length. You won't be able to use the chopsticks if the tip of one stick protrudes beyond the other.
4. When picking up food, the lower chopstick should remain still. Only the upper chopstick should move, with the thumb as the axis.

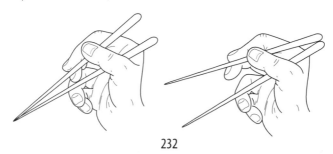

Four Major Holidays of the Year

January 1	New Year's Day (celebrated 1 to 3 days)
late January–early February	Chinese New Year (3 days to 1 week)
May 1–3	International Labor Day (3 days)
October 1–3	National Day (3 days to 1 week)

The above are holidays that are celebrated by nearly everyone in China. Although some are officially listed as three-day holidays, plan for them to be disruptive to schedules for at least a week or more. Don't plan anything two days before and a week after the first day.

The following schedule gives the Chinese holidays to be celebrated in 2007. Besides the major holidays, it includes *partial holidays* for particular groups of people. Business meetings may or may not be affected by partial holidays.

January 1	New Year's Day
February 18	Chinese New Year or Spring Festival
March 4	Lantern Festival (dumplings)
March 8	International Women's Day (all women get a half day off)
May 1	International Labor Day (3 days)
June 1	International Children's Day (all persons ages 14 to 20 get a half day off)
June 19	Dragon Boat Festival (work day)
August 1	Army Day (for all armed forces personnel)
September 25	Mid-Autumn Festival (moon cake)
October 1	National Day (1 week)
October 19	Double Nine Festival (for senior-aged people)

| # The Chinese Zodiac

In China the New Year is assigned to an animal. According to tradition, Buddha promised gifts to all animals who would pay him homage. Only twelve animals came to honor Buddha, so to favor these twelve animals, each was given one of the twelve years of the Chinese zodiac. Persons born during a given animal's year are said to inherit the distinctive characteristics of that animal. The signs repeat every twelve years:

Animal	Solar Birth Year				
Rat	1900	1912	1924	1936	1948
	1960	1972	1984	1996	2008
Ox	1901	1913	1925	1937	1949
	1961	1973	1985	1997	2009
Tiger	1902	1914	1926	1938	1950
	1962	1974	1986	1998	2010
Rabbit	1903	1915	1927	1939	1951
	1963	1975	1987	1999	2011
Dragon	1904	1916	1928	1940	1952
	1964	1976	1988	2000	2012
Snake	1905	1917	1929	1941	1953
	1965	1977	1989	2001	2013
Horse	1906	1918	1930	1942	1954
	1966	1978	1990	2002	2014
Sheep	1907	1919	1931	1943	1955
	1967	1979	1991	2003	2015
Monkey	1908	1920	1932	1944	1956
	1968	1980	1992	2004	2016
Rooster	1909	1921	1933	1945	1957
	1969	1981	1993	2005	2017
Dog	1910	1922	1934	1946	1958
	1970	1982	1994	2006	2018
Boar	1911	1923	1935	1947	1959
	1971	1983	1995	2007	2019

The map on the following page contains the provinces, regions, and most-traveled-to cities of eastern and central China. The numbers indicate provinces, autonomous regions, and independent cities; the letters indicate the exact location of major cities within these provinces and regions. Cities that are independent areas (and not part of any province or region) have both a letter and a number. Examples would be Beijing in the northern section of the map (F and 5) and Hong Kong in the south (S and 26).

Not included on the map are **Inner Mongolia** (an autonomous region in northern China), **Xinjiang Uygur** and **Tibet** (autonomous regions in western China), and **Qinghai** (a province in western China). Few Americans travel to these regions for business purposes, and western China has few significant cities.

Taiwan (25 on the map) is governed by the Republic of China (ROC), but it is still considered by the People's Republic of China (PRC) to be part of the territory of mainland China.

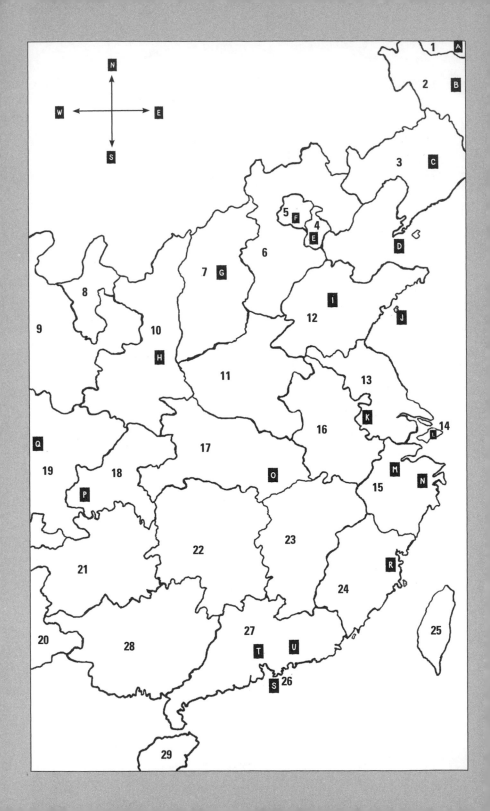

Cities (and their provinces)	Map location
Beijing (independent)	F
Changchun (Jilin)	B
Chengdu (Sichuan)	Q
Chongqing (independent)	P
Dalian (Liaoning)	D
Fuzhou (Fujian)	R
Guangzhou (Guangdong)	T
Hangzhou (Zheijiang)	M
Harbin (Heilongjiang)	A
Hong Kong (independent)	S
Jinan (Shandong)	I
Nanjing (Jiangsu)	K
Ningbo (Zheijiang)	N
Qingdao (Shandong)	J
Shanghai (independent)	L
Shenyang (Liaoning)	C
Shenzhen (Guangdong)	U
Taiyuan (Shanxi)	G
Tianjin (independent)	E
Wuhan (Hubei)	D
Xi'an (Shanxi)	H

Provinces, independent cities (I), and autonomous regions (A)	Map location
Anhui	16
Beijing (I)	5
Chongqing (I)	18
Fujian	24
Gansu	9
Guangdong	27
Guanxi (A)	28
Guizhou	21
Hainan	29
Hebei	6
Heilongjiang	1
Henan	11
Hong Kong (I)	26
Hubei	17
Hunan	22
Jiangsu	13
Jiangxi	23
Jilin	2
Liaoning	3
Ningxia (A)	8
Shaanxi	10
Shandong	12
Shanghai (I)	14
Shanxi	7
Sichuan	19
Tianjin (I)	4
Yunnan	20
Zheijiang	15

| **Temperatures and Rainfall in China**

Note: All temperatures in degrees Fahrenheit, and rainfall in inches

City	Avg High Jan	Avg Low Jan	Avg High July	Avg Low July	Annual Rainfall
Beijing	33	13	87	69	21.7 in
Changchun	12	-9	81	64	22.9 in
Changsha	45	33	92	76	52.9 in
Chengdu	50	37	86	72	36.9 in
Chongqing	51	42	92	76	42.0 in
Dalian	30	17	80	69	30.0 in
Guangzhou	65	50	91	77	65.8 in
Hangzhou	46	33	92	77	55.9 in
Harbin	10	-12	85	67	21.4 in
Jinan	38	22	91	74	24.4 in
Luoyang	43	25	91	74	23.4 in
Nanchang	48	36	93	78	63.6 in
Nanjing	44	29	90	76	37.6 in
Ningbo	48	37	87	76	55.0 in
Shanghai	47	32	90	76	38.5 in
Shenyang	22	1	85	69	19.7 in
Shenzhen	67	51	90	77	73.0 in
Shijiazhuang	38	18	89	72	20.7 in
Taiyuan	34	8	86	65	16.4 in
Tianjin	34	17	88	72	20.2 in
Wuhan	46	31	92	78	47.2 in
Xi'an	42	25	93	73	29.1 in

| # Air Mileage Between Key Cities (in Miles)

City	Beijing	Shanghai	Guangzhou
Beijing	X	665	1,176
Changchun	534	899	1,591
Chengdu	943	1,031	769
Chongqing	906	894	607
Dalian	289	532	1,199
Fushun	413	747	1,434
Guangzhou	1,176	754	X
Hangzhou	710	114	640
Harbin	656	1,041	1,735
Jinan	228	455	963
Nanjing	561	168	704
Ningbo	824	96	587
Shanghai	665	X	754
Shenyang	390	739	1,419
Shenzhen	390	739	1,419
Tianjin	70	597	1,131
Ürümqi	1,563	2,072	2,039
Wuhan	657	429	519
Xi'an	569	760	814

Appendix 10 | The Most Populous Cities in Mainland China

1.	Shanghai	13,278,500
2.	Beijing	7,209,900
3.	Wuhan	4,104,300
4.	Chengdu	4,064,700
5.	Tianjin	3,945,900
6.	Shenyang	3,527,800
7.	Xi'an	3,480,600
8.	Chongqing	3,378,900
9.	Guangzhou	3,244,900
10.	Harbin	3,129,300
11.	Nanjing	2,870,200
12.	Taiyuan	2,690,500
13.	Changchun	2,337,000
14.	Zhengzhou	2,052,700
15.	Guiyang	2,040,200
16.	Jinan	1,961,500
17.	Dalian	1,925,200
18.	Changsha	1,891,000
19.	Hangzhou	1,881,500
20.	Shijiazhuang	1,683,800
21.	Nanchang	1,657,900
22.	Jilin	1,625,700
23.	Tangshan	1,600,600
24.	Qingdao	1,584,300
25.	Ürümqi	1,424,300
26.	Luoyang	1,417,200
27.	Xinyang	1,412,300
28.	Lanzhou	1,409,200
29.	Fushun	1,409,000
30.	Hefei	1,362,900

Other common destinations:

58.	Shenzhen	752,200
64.	Ningbo	689,300

Source: *www.travelchinaguide.com/cityguides/zhejiang/ningbo/*

Appendix 11 | Recommended Hotels for the Canton Fair

Five-Star Hotels
Guangzhou Asia International
Sheraton Dongguan Hotel
Fontainebleau Hotel
Dongguan Jia Hua Grand Hotel
The Grand Bay View Hotel, Zhuhai
Foshan Hotel
Phoenix City Hotel
Chime Long Hotel
Dongguan Chinese Hotel

Four-Star Hotels
Ever Profit Hotel
Chancheng Hotel
Liu Hua Hotel
Holiday Inn City Centre Guangzhou
Bai Yun Hotel
Hotel Landmark Canton
Guangzhou MEIYI Hotel
Foshan Huaqiao Hotel
Guangdong Hotel
Panyu Hotel
Pearl Garden Hotel
Dongguan Hotel
Zengcheng Hotel
Golden City Hotel
Jin Du Hotel

Three-Star Hotels
Overseas Chinese Friendship Hotel
Nanzhou Hotel
Li Yun Hotel
Riverview Hotel
New Mainland Hotel
Xinyue Hotel
Guangxuan Hotel

| **Average Annual Wage by Province**

Region	Total	Agriculture, Forestry, Animal Husbandry, and Fishing	Mining	Manufacturing	Construction	Transport, Storage, and Post
National total	**14040**	**6969**	**13682**	**18752**	**11478**	**15973**
Beijing	25312	14980	18858	37112	16730	19977
Tianjin	18648	13347	23605	26085	19609	23748
Hebei	11189	4857	14057	17582	9098	12777
Shanxi	10729	7787	12871	12468	9169	13894
Inner Mongolia	11279	6832	9760	17942	8297	13604
Liaoning	13008	4960	13756	18559	9660	14688
Jilin	11081	5512	11859	15206	8716	10909
Heilongjiang	11038	5373	13466	15702	10641	12784
Shanghai	27304	18706	44197	32330	24591	25903
Jiangsu	15712	7468	14530	25000	13167	17031
Zhejiang	21367	16583	13994	34733	15982	22718
Anhui	10581	5985	12699	13563	8531	9473
Fujian	14310	7974	10858	20562	13779	18181
Jiangxi	10521	5534	9421	12707	9220	14011
Shandong	12567	8643	17802	17681	10028	16124
Henan	10749	6155	14339	14570	9370	12556
Hubei	10692	5340	11556	14247	9926	11827
Hunan	12221	5357	9189	15022	9328	12565
Guangdong	19986	8997	12961	28574	14608	25936
Guangxi	11953	6796	10865	17571	10604	13999
Hainan	10397	4762	8264	15928	9190	15571
Chongqing	12425	8877	9725	16372	10028	12506
Sichuan	12441	8988	10613	15303	9255	13171
Guizhou	11037	8563	11556	18801	8942	13280
Yunnan	12870	9803	10861	18490	10475	13810
Tibet	26931	19113	16284	23092	17805	22759
Shaanxi	11461	8230	12534	16218	9926	14506
Gansu	12307	8971	12205	17544	9303	14843
Qinghai	15356	10836	14930	21364	10694	18227
Ningxia	12981	8297	14573	18793	10893	15341
Xinjiang	13255	9005	19978	17724	11619	17767

and Region (2003) *RMB in current prices (yuan)*

Information Transmission, Computer Service, and Software	Wholesale and Retail Trade	Hotels and Restaurants	Financial Intermediation	Real Estate	Leasing and Business Services	Scientific Research, Technical Services, and Geological Prospecting	Education
32244	10939	11083	22457	17182	16501	20636	14399
53010	23088	16530	61713	26064	25742	34898	28565
33785	15606	12430	26295	21253	13514	24545	19226
23494	6824	7900	15237	10832	9225	16699	11100
17953	6178	6250	15103	9472	8353	13109	11648
17367	7867	7516	14060	10858	12511	14060	13383
35486	10466	10123	20171	13394	11915	17600	13704
21777	6935	8357	15559	11596	11824	14140	12950
26318	8400	8528	18407	11142	9069	14084	13808
62821	25038	21168	42544	32802	22990	30928	26601
32533	11452	11869	24173	16897	15931	23744	16549
44263	20288	13516	31578	22692	20137	28627	25677
19158	6163	7302	14475	11128	8483	13348	11436
33158	13375	10333	26245	16582	14538	19913	15029
16831	7782	8313	15390	9873	10783	12804	10986
24660	8006	9249	19924	14269	12805	17264	13342
19377	7169	7917	16595	11159	10321	14986	10774
16517	6923	7134	14539	10616	9943	14610	12098
21361	10337	9638	18159	12959	13380	14853	13309
42966	18296	14778	33426	22312	21306	32963	20449
23783	8558	8001	17341	12596	10396	14944	11344
27898	8810	8352	19979	12017	10607	11709	13353
25298	10497	9412	22300	12174	10805	14478	12865
23069	10055	9192	20550	12688	12559	19913	12825
18426	8630	8581	16121	10396	11884	14090	10597
19343	11068	8793	15133	12694	14861	14827	13391
45446	14036	13251	32525	20670	15988	31626	28138
26772	7290	7654	17032	10931	9853	14977	12598
13104	7397	7461	13991	11178	10345	14470	13534
24594	9986	11811	19235	14024	12874	21917	16473
26867	9268	7918	19532	10678	11282	13876	15115
23338	13082	10337	20680	13327	12666	16201	15167

Appendix 13 | Metric Conversion Chart—Approximations

When You Know	Multiply By	To Find
Length		
millimeters	0.04	inches
centimeters	0.39	inches
meters	3.28	feet
meters	1.09	yards
kilometers	0.62	miles
inches	25.4	millimeter
inches	2.54	centimeters
feet	30.48	centimeters
yards	0.94	meters
miles	1.61	kilometers
Area		
square centimeters	0.16	square inches
square meters	1.2	square yards
square kilometers	0.39	square miles
hectares	2.47	acres
square inches	6.45	square centimeters
square feet	0.09	square meters
square yards	0.84	square meters
square miles	2.6	square kilo
acres	0.4	hectares
Mass and Weight		
grams	0.035	ounces
kilograms	2.21	pounds
tons (100 kg)	1.1	short tons
ounces	28.35	grams
pounds	0.45	kilograms
short tons (2,000 lb.)	0.91	tons

Appendix 13 | Metric Conversion Chart

When You Know	Multiply By	To Find
Volume		
milliliters	0.2	teaspoons
milliliters	0.06	tablespoons
milliliters	0.03	fluid ounces
liters	4.23	cups
liters	2.12	pints
liters	1.06	quarts
liters	0.26	gallons
cubic meters	35.32	cubic feet
cubic meters	1.35	cubic yards
teaspoons	4.93	milliliters
tablespoons	14.78	milliliters
fluid ounces	29.57	milliliters
cups	0.24	liters
pints	0.47	liters
quarts	0.95	liters
gallons	3.79	liters
Volume		
cubic meters	35.3	cubic feet
cubic yards	0.76	cubic meters
Speed		
kilometers per hour	0.62	miles per hour
miles per hour	1.61	kilometers per hour
Temperature		
Celsius	9/5, +32	Fahrenheit
Fahrenheit	-32, 5/9 × remainder	Celsius

Appendix 13 | Metric Conversion Chart

The following temperatures are ones that are frequently encountered:

0°C	Freezing point of water (32°F)
10°C	A warm winter day (50°F)
20°C	A mild spring day (68°F)
30°C	A hot summer day (86°F)
37°C	Normal body temperature (98.6°F)
40°C	Heat-wave conditions (104°F)
100°C	Boiling point of water (212°F)

Appendix 14 | Container Dimensions

	Length	Width	Height	Total Cu. Ft.
Small Container (20')	20'	8'	8.5'	1,360
Large Container (40')	40'	8'	8.5'	2,720

These Web sites are good starting points for researching potential investment opportunities in China.

http://irasia.com—Broad access to annual reports, financial filings and general news about regional companies.

www.listedcompany.com—Much of the same, but also allows you to monitor current and recent IPOs.

www.hkex.com.hk—Home page of the Hong Kong Stock Exchange. Retrieve complete list of Chinese H shares and Red Chips; performance data; stock charts; company announcements and regulatory filings. Also has links to the Shanghai and Shenzhen stock exchanges.

http://ses.com.sg—Home page of the Singapore Stock Exchange. Convenient links to company profiles and market data. Investors can register for free research from local brokerage firms such as Kim-Eng Securities and DBS Vickers.

www.sse.com.cn/sseportal/en_us/ps/home.shtml—Home page of Shanghai Stock Exchange. Posts data on the B-share market.

http://shkonline.com/eng/startpage_main.jhtml—Shkonline.com features market data for investing in the region, including China.

http://home.boom.com.hk/index.html—Boom.com, the home page of a Hong Kong securities company, provides information on stock trading in the region.

http://kimeng.com/home.htm—The home page of Kim Eng, a leading Asian securities and investment broker.

Source: The *Wall Street Journal*

247

State Commissions

State Commission of Science, Technology, and Industry for National Defense
A8 Fuchen Lu, Haidian District, Beijing 100037, China
Beijing 2940 Post Box
Minister: Zhang Yunchuan
Tel: (86-10) 6851-6733
Fax: (86-10) 6851-6732
www.costind.gov.cn (Chinese only)

National Development and Reform Commission
38 Yuetannanjie, Xicheng District, Beijing 100824, China
Minister: Ma Kai
Tel: (86-10) 6850-2000
Fax: (86-10) 6850-2929
www.endrc.gov.cn

State Economic and Trade Commission
26 Xuanwumen Xidajie, Xuanwu District, Beijing 100053, China
Minister: Li Rongrong
Tel: (86-10) 6319-2299
Fax: (86-10) 6319-2177
www.setc.gov.cn/english/index_e.htm

Ministries

Ministry of Agriculture
11 Nongzhanguan Nanli, Chaoyang District, Beijing 100026, China
Minister: Du Qinglin
Tel: (86-10) 6419-3366
Fax: (86-10) 6419-2468
www.agri.gov.cn (Chinese only)

| **Information and Contacts**

Ministry of Communications
11 Jianguomennei Dajie, Dongcheng District, Beijing 100736, China
Minister: Zhang Chunxian
Tel: (86-10) 6529-2513
Fax: (86-10) 6529-2427
www.moc.gov.cn (Chinese only)

Ministry of Construction
9 Sanlihe Lu, Baiwanzhuang, Haidian District, Beijing 100835, China
Minister: Wang Guangtao
Tel: (86-10) 5893-3575
Fax: (86-10) 5893-4215
www.cin.gov.cn (Chinese only)

Ministry of Culture
10 Chaoyangmen Beijie, Dongcheng District, Beijing 10020, China
Minister: Sun Jiazheng
Tel: (86-10) 6555-1208
Fax: (86-10) 6555-1193
www.ccnt.gov.cn (Chinese only)

Ministry of Education
37 Damucang Hutong, Xidan, Xicheng District, Beijing 100816, China
Minister: Zhou Ji
Tel: (86-10) 6609-6114
Fax: (86-10) 6601-1049
www.moe.gov.cn/english

Ministry of Finance
3 Nansanxiang, Sanlihe, Xicheng District, Beijing 100820, China
Minister: Jin Renqing
Tel: (86-10) 6855-1114
Fax: (86-10) 6855-1627
www.mof.gov.cn/english/english.htm

Appendix 16 | Information and Contacts

Ministry of Foreign Affairs
2 Chaoyangmen Nandajie, Dongcheng District, Beijing 100701, China
Minister: Li Zhaoxing
Tel: (86-10) 6596-1114
Fax: (86-10) 6596-1138
www.fmprc.gov.cn/eng/default.htm

Ministry of Commerce
2 Dongchang'an Jie, Beijing 100731, China
Minister: Bo Xilai
Tel: (86-10) 6512-1919
Fax: (86-10) 6559-9340
http://english.mofcom.gov.cn

Ministry of Public Health
1 Xizhimenwai Nanlu, Xicheng District, Beijing 100044, China
Minister: Wu Yi
Tel: (86-10) 6879-2114
Fax: (86-10) 6879-2024
www.moh.gov.cn (Chinese only)

Ministry of Information Industry
13 Xichang'anjie, Beijing 100804, China
Minister: Wang Xudong
Tel: (86-10) 6601-4249
Fax: (86-10) 6201-4249
www.mii.gov.cn (Chinese only)

Ministry of Justice
10 Chaoyangmen Nandajie, Chaoyang District, Beijing 100020, China
Minister: Wu Aiying
Tel: (86-10) 6520-5114
Fax: (86-10) 6520-5345
www.legalinfo.gov.cn/english/englishindex.htm

| **Information and Contacts**

Ministry of Labor and Social Security
12 Hepingli Zhongjie, Dongcheng District, Beijing 100716, China
Minister: Tian Cheng Ping
Tel: (86-10) 8420-1114
Fax: (86-10) 8422-3056
www.molss.gov.cn (Chinese only, English under construction)

Ministry of Land and Resources
No. 3 Guanyingyuan Xiqu, Xicheng District, Beijing 100035, China
Minister: Sun Wensheng
Tel: (86-10) 6655-8001
Fax: (86-10) 6612-7005
www.mlr.gov.cn/pub/mlr/english/default.htm

Ministry of Personnel
7 Hepingli Zhongjie, Dongchen District, Beijing 100013, China
Minister: Zhang Bolin
Tel: (86-10) 6492-1115
Fax: (86-10) 8422-3240
www.mop.gov.cn/Desktop.aspx?PATH=rsbww/sy/e_rsbjj

Ministry of Public Security
14 Dongchang'anjie, Beijing 100741, China
Minister: Zhou Yongkang
Tel: (86-10) 6520-2114
Fax: (86-10) 6524-1596
www.mps.gov.cn (Chinese only)

Ministry of Railways
10 Fuxing Lu, Haidian District, Beijing 100844, China
Minister: Fu Zhihuan
Tel: (86-10) 5184-1206
Fax: (86-10) 6324-2150
www.china-mor.gov.cn (Chinese only)

Ministry of Science and Technology
15 Fuxinglu, Haidian District, Beijing 100862, China
Minister: Xu Guanhua
Tel: (86-10) 5888-1234
Fax: (86-10) 6851-5006
www.most.gov.cn/eng/

Ministry of Water Resources
2 Baiguanglu Ertiao, Xuanwu District, Beijing 100053, China
Minister: Wang Shucheng
Tel: (86-10) 6320-2114
Fax: (86-10) 6320-3070
http://www.mwr.gov.cn/english/index.htm

Bureaus and Administrations Directly under the State Council

Bureau of Government Offices Administration
22 Xi'anmen Dajie, Beijing 100017, China
Director: Jiao Huancheng
Tel: (86-10) 6603-6884
Fax: (86-10) 6309-6382
www.ggj.gov.cn (Chinese only)

General Administration of Civil Aviation of China
155 Dongsi Xidajie, Beijing 100710, China
Director: Yang Yuan Yuan
Tel: (86-10) 6428-0972
Fax: (86-10) 6401-3663
www.caac.gov.cn (Chinese only, English under construction)

| **Information and Contacts**

General Administration of Customs
6 Jianguomennei Dajie, Beijing 100730, China
Director: Mu Xinsheng
Tel: (86-10) 6519-4114
Fax: (86-10) 6519-5149
http://english.customs.gov.cn/default.aspx

National Tourism Administration
Jia 9 Jianguomennei Dajie, Beijing 100740, China
Director: He Guangwei
Tel: (86-10) 6520-1114
Fax: (86-10) 6512-2096
www.cnta.com/lyen/index.asp

State Administration for Industry and Commerce
8 Sanlihe Donglu, Xicheng District, Beijing 100820, China
Director: Wang Zhongfu
Tel: (86-10) 6803-2233
Fax: (86-10) 6802-0848
http://gsyj.saic.gov.cn/wcm/WCMData/pub/saic/english/default.htm

State Administration for Religious Affairs
32 Beisantiao, Jiaodaokou, Dongcheng District, Beijing 100007, China
Director: Ye Xiaowen
Tel: (86-10) 6402-3355
Fax: (86-10) 6601-3565
www.sara.gov.cn (Chinese only)

State Administration of Radio, Film, and Television
2 Fuxingmenwai Dajie, Beijing 100866, China
Minister: Wang Taihua
Tel: (86-10) 6609-3114
Fax: (86-10) 6609-2437
www.sarft.gov.cn (Chinese only)

Appendix 16 | Information and Contacts

State General Administration for Quality Supervision and Inspection and Quarantine
A10 Chaowai Dajie, Chaoyang District, Beijing 100020, China
Director: Li Changjiang
Tel: (86-10) 8840-8170/71/72
Fax: (86-10) 6599-4304
www.aqsiq.gov.cn (Chinese only)

State Administration of Taxation
5 Yangfangdian Xilu, Haidian District, Beijing 100038, China
Director: Xie Xuren
Tel: (86-10) 6341-7114
Fax: (86-10) 6341-7321
www.chinatax.gov.cn (Chinese only)

State Food and Drug Administration
Jia 38 Beilishilu, Xicheng District, Beijing 100810, China
Director: Shao Liming
Tel: Drugs (86-10) 6831-3344
Tel: Food (86-10) 6717-2978
Fax: (86-10) 6831-0909
www.sfda.gov.cn/eng

State Environmental Protection Administration
115 Xizhimennei Nanxiaojie, Beijing 100035, China
Minister: Zho Shengxian
Tel: (86-10) 6615-1780
Fax: (86-10) 6615-1768
www.sepa.gov.cn/english

| **Information and Contacts**

State Forestry Administration
18 Hepingli Dongjie, Beijing 100714, China
Director: Zhou Shengxian
Tel: (86-10) 8423-8302
Fax: (86-10) 6421-3193
www.forestry.gov.cn (Chinese only)

State Intellectual Property Office
6 Xituchenglu, Jimenqiao, Haidian District, Beijing 100088, China
Director: Tain Lipu
Tel: (86-10) 6208-3114
Fax: (86-10) 6201-9307
www.sipo.gov.cn/sipo_English/default.htm

General Administration of Press and Publication
85 Dongsi Nandajie, Dongcheng District, Beijing 100703, China
Director: Shi Zongyuan
Tel: (86-10) 6512-4433
Fax: (86-10) 6512-7875
www.gapp.gov.cn (Chinese only)

General Administration of Sport
9 Tiyuguanlu, Chongwen District, Beijing 100763, China
Minister: Liu Pong
Tel: (86-10) 8718-2299
Fax: (86-10) 6711-1154
www.sport.gov.cn (Chinese only)

National Bureau of Statistics
75 Yuetannanjie, Sanlihe, Beijing 100826, China
Director: Li Deshui
Tel: (86-10) 6857-6320
Fax: (86-10) 6858-0964
www.stats.gov.cn/english/index.htm

Appendix 16 | Information and Contacts

General Office of the State Council
22 Xianmen Dajie, Beijing 100017, China
Secretary General: Hua Jianmin
Tel: (86-10) 6309-5756
Fax: (86-10) 6610-6016

Hong Kong and Macau Affairs Office
77 Yuetannanjie, Beijing 100045, China
Director: Liao Hui
Tel: (86-10) 6857-9977
Fax: (86-10) 6857-6639
www.hmo.gov.cn (Chinese only)

China Internet Information Center
225 Chaoyangmenwai, Dongcheng District, Beijing 100010, China
Director: Zhao Qizheng
Tel: (86-10) 8652-1199
Fax: (86-10) 6559-2364
www.china.org.cn

Legislative Affairs Office
9 Wenjinjie, Beijing 100017, China
Director: Cao Kangtai
Tel: (86-10) 6309-7599
Fax: (86-10) 6309-7699
www.chinalaw.gov.cn/indexEN.jsp

Overseas Chinese Affairs Office
35 Fuwaidajie, Beijing 100037, China
Director: Chen Yujie
Tel: (86-10) 6832-7530
Fax: (86-10) 6832-7477
www.gqb.gov.cn (Chinese only)

| **Information and Contacts**

Research Office
Zhongnanhai, Beijing 100017, China
Director: Wei Liqun
Tel: (86-10) 6309-7785

Office for Restructuring Economic System
22 Xi'anmen Dajie, Beijing 100017, China
Director: Wang Qishan
Tel: (86-10) 6309-9065
Fax: (86-10) 6601-4562

China Meteorological Administration
46 Baishiqiaolu, Haidian District, Beijing 100081, China
Director: Qin Dahe
Tel: (86-10) 6840-6114
Fax: (86-10) 6217-4797
http://211.147.16.25/ywwz

China Securities Regulatory Commission
19A Jinrongdajie, Xicheng District, Beijing 100032, China
Director: Liu Mingkang
Tel: (86-10) 8066-1000
Fax: (86-10) 6621-0206
www.csrc.gov.cn/en/homepage/index_en.jsp

Chinese Academy of Engineering
3 Fuxinglu, Haidian District, Beijing 100038, China
President: Xu Kuangdi
Tel: (86-10) 6857-0320
Fax: (86-10) 6851-9694
www.cae.cn/english/index.jsp

Chinese Academy of Sciences
52 Sanlihe, Xicheng District, Beijing 100864, China
President: Lu Yongxiang
Tel: (86-10) 6859-7114
Fax: (86-10) 6851-1095
http://english.cas.cn/Eng2003/page/home.asp

Chinese Academy of Social Sciences
5 Jiannei Dajie, Beijing 100732, China
President: Chen Kuiyuan
Tel: (86-10) 6513-7744
Fax: (86-10) 6513-8154
www.cass.net.cn (Chinese only)

Development Research Center
225 Chaoyangmen Dajie, Beijing 100010, China
Director: Hua Jianmin
Tel: (86-10) 6523-0008
Fax: (86-10) 6523-6060
www.drc.gov.cn (Chinese only, English under construction)

National School of Administration
6 Changchunqiaolu, Haidian District, Beijing 100089, China
President: Wang Zhongyu
Tel: (86-10) 6842-7894
Fax: (86-10) 6842-7895
www.nsa.gov.cn (Chinese only)

China Seismological Bureau
63 Fuxing Lu, Haidian District, Beijing 100036, China
Director: Song Ruixiang
Tel: (86-10) 6821-5522
Fax: (86-10) 6821-0995
www.csi.ac.cn (Chinese only)

State Administration of Foreign Exchange
18 Fuchenglu, Beijing 100037, China
Director: Mr. Hu Xiaolian
Tel: (86-10) 6840-2147/2231
Fax: (86-10) 6840-2147
www.safe.gov.cn/model_safe_en/index.jsp?id=6

State Administration of Traditional Chinese Medicine
Building 13, Bajiazhuang Dongli, Chaoyang District, Beijing 100026, China
Director: Ms. She Jing
Tel: (86-10) 6506-3322
Fax: (86-10) 6595-0776
www.satcm.gov.cn/english_satcm/eindex.htm

State Administration of Cultural Heritage
10 Chao Yang Men Bei Da Jie, Chaoiyang District, Beijing 100020, China
Director: Zhang Wenbin
Tel: (86-10) 6555-1554
Fax: (86-10) 6555-1555

State Administration of Foreign Experts Affairs
1 Nandajie, Zhong Quan Cuen, Beijing 100873, China
Director: Wan Xueyuan
Tel: (86-10) 6894-8899
Fax: (86-10) 6846-8006
www.safea.gov.cn/english

State Bureau of Surveying and Mapping
9 Sanlihelu, Baiwanzhuang, Beijing 100830, China
Director: Lu Xinshe
Tel: (86-10) 6832-1893
Fax: (86-10) 6831-1564
www.sbsm.gov.cn (Chinese only)

State Grain Administration
11A, Muxudi Belili, Xincheng District, Beijing 100038, China
Director: Nie Zhengbang
Tel: (86-10) 6390-6078
Fax: (86-10) 6390-6058
www.chinagrain.gov.cn (Chinese only)

China National Light Industry Council
Yi 22 Fuwaidajie, Beijing 100083, China
Director: Chen Shineng
Tel: (86-10) 6113/6112
Fax: (86-10) 6839-6264
www.clii.com.cn/english

China Building Materials Information
46 Sanlihelu, Xicheng District, Beijing 100823, China
Director: Zhang Renwei
Tel: (86-10) 6859-4965
Fax: (86-10) 6851-3867
www.cbminfo.com

China Iron and Steel Association
46 Dongsi Xidajie, Dongcheng District, Beijing 100711, China
Director: Wu Xichun
Tel: (86-10) 6513-3322/1935
Fax: (86-10) 6513-0074
www.chinaesteel.com/mmi_en/index.htm

State Oceanic Administration
1 Fuxingmenwai Dajie, Beijing 100860, China
Director: Sun Zhihui
Tel: (86-10) 6803-7660
Fax: (86-10) 6801-9791
www.soa.gov.cn (Chinese only)

China Petroleum and Chemical Industry Association
Building 16, 4 District, Anhuili, Yayuncun, Chaoyang District, Beijing 100723, China
Director: Tan Zhuzhou
Tel: (86-10) 8488-5100/5430/5056
Fax: (86-10) 8488-5087
www.cpcia.org

State Postal Bureau
131 Xuan Wu Men Xi Da Jie District, Beijing 100031, China
Director: Liu Andong
Tel: (86-10) 6606-9955
Fax: (86-10) 6641-9711
www.chinapost.gov.cn/English/index.htm

China National Textile Industry Council
12 Dongchang'anjie, Beijing 100742, China
Director: Du Yuzhou
Tel: (86-10) 8522-9207/9205/9217
Fax: (86-10) 8522-9283

State Tobacco Monopoly Bureau
26 West Xuanwumen Avenue, Xuanwu District, Beijing 100053, China
Director: Jiang Chenkang
Tel: (86-10) 6360-5852/5782
Fax: (86-10) 6360-5036
www.tobacco.gov.cn (Chinese only)

Associations and Corporations

All-China Federation of Industry and Commerce
93 Beiheyan Dajie, Beijing 100006, China
Chairman: Huang Mengfu
Tel: (86-10) 6513-6677 Ext. 2233, 2234
Fax: (86-10) 6513-1769
www.chinachamber.org.cn

Appendix 16 | Information and Contacts

China General Chamber of Commerce (co-located with CCPIT, see below)
1 Fuxingmenwai Street, Beijing 100834, China
Chairman: Su Qiuchen
Tel: (86-10) 6839-1247
Fax: (86-10) 6851-1370
www.china-retailers.com.cn/english

China Council for the Promotion of International Trade (CCPIT)
1 Fuxingmenwai Street, Beijing 100860, China
President: Yu Xiaosong
Tel: (86-10) 6801-3344
Fax:(86-10) 6801-1370
www.ccpit.org/servlet/infosystem.ServletGoToInfosystemHome

China Huaneng Group
40 Xue Yuan Nan Lu, Haidian District, Beijing 100088, China
President: Li Xiaopong
Tel: (86-10) 6229-1888
Fax: (86-10) 6229-1899
www.chng.com.cn/minisite/en/index.html

China International Trust and Investment Corporation
Capital Mansion, 6 Xinyuan Nanlu, Chaoyangqu, Beijing 100004, China
President: Wang Jun
Tel: (86-10) 6466-0088 8486-8718
Fax: (86-10) 6466-1186
www.citic.com

China Metals Information Network
Yi 12 Fuxing Lu, Xicheng, Beijing 100814, China
President: Kang Yi
Tel: (86-10) 6396-6393 6397-1807
Fax: (86-10) 6396-5360
www.antaike.com/gj/index.asp

Appendix 16 | Information and Contacts

China National Offshore Oil Corporation
P.O. Box 4705, 6 Dongzhimenwai Xiaojie, Beijing 100027, China
President: Fu Chengyu
Tel: (86-10) 8452-1071
Fax: (86-10) 8452-1080
www.cnooc.com.cn/defaulten.asp

China National Petroleum Corporation
6 Liupukang, Xicheng District, Beijing 100724, China
President: Chen Geng
Tel: (86-10) 6209-4100
Fax: (86-10) 6209-4806
www.cnpc.com.cn/english/index.htm

China North Industries Corporation
Guang An Men Nan Da Jie Jia 12, Beijing 100053, China
President: Zang Guoqin
Tel: (86-10) 6352-9988
Fax: (86-10) 6354-0398
www.norinco.com.cn/c1024/english/index.html

China Petroleum and Chemical Corporation
6 Hui Xin Dong Jie Jia, Beijing 100029, China
President: Chen Tonghai
Tel: (86-10) 6499-9936
Fax: (86-10) 6421-8356
http://english.sinopec.com/index.jsp

China State Construction International
12F 37 Maizidianjie,Chaoyiang District, Beijing 100026, China
President: Yi Jun
Tel: (86-10) 8527-6677
Fax: (86-10) 8527-5566
www.chinaconstruction.com/en/main.htm

China State Shipbuilding Corporation
5 Yuetanbeijie, Xicheng District, Beijing 100861, China
President: Li Changyin
Tel: (86-10) 6803-8833 6803-9205
Fax: (86-10)6803-1579

China Everbright Group
6 Fu Xing Men Wai Street, Everbright Building, Beijing 100045, China
President: Zang Qiutao
Tel: (86-10) 6856-0088
Fax: (86-10) 6856-1121
www.ebchina.com/english/eb-e.html

PICC Property and Casualty Company Limited
#69 Xuan Wu Men Dong He Yan Jie, Beijing 100052, China
President: Tang Yunxiang
Tel: (86-10) 6315-6688
Fax: (86-10) 6303-3589
www.picc.com.cn/en/index.shtml

Chambers of Commerce/Trade Associations

American Association for Manufacturing Technology (AMT)
Rm. 2507 Silver Tower, 2 Dongsanhuan North Road, Chaoyang District, Beijing 100027, China
Tel: (86-10) 6410-7374, 6410-7375/76
Fax: (86-10) 6410-7334
www.AMTonline.org

American Chamber of Commerce in Beijing
Charlie Martin, President
Mike Furst, Executive Director
Suite 1903 China Resources Building, 8 Jianguomenbei Avenue, Beijing 100005, China
Tel: (86-10) 8519-1920
Fax: (86-10) 8519-1910
www.amcham-china.org.cn

| **Information and Contacts**

American Soybean Association International Marketing
Phillip W. Laney, Representative
China World Tower 2, Room 902, Beijing 100004, China
Tel: (86-10) 6505-1830, 6505-1831, 6505-3533
Fax: (86-10) 6505-2201
www.asasoya.org

Association of Equipment Manufacturers (formerly Construction Industry Manufacturers Association)
No. 6 Southern Capital Gymnasium Road, Room 458, Office Tower New Century Hotel,
    Beijing 100044, China
Tel: (86-10) 6849-2403
Fax: (86-10) 6849-2404
www.cm-1.com/index.cfm?lan=E

U.S.-China Business Council
Patrick Powers, Chief Representative
CITIC Building, Suite 26D, Beijing 100004, China
Tel: (86-10) 6592-0727
Fax: (86-10) 6512-5854
www.uschina.org

U.S. Grains Council
Todd Meyer, Director
China World Tower 2, Room 901, Beijing 100004, China
Tel: (86-10) 6505-1314, 6505-2320
Fax: (86-10) 6505-0236
www.grains.org

U.S. Wheat Associates
Zhao Shipu, Director
China World Tower 2, Room 903, Beijing 100004, China
Tel: (86-10) 6505-1278, 6505-3866
Fax: (86-10) 6505-5138
www.uswheat.org

Appendix 16 | Information and Contacts

United States Information Technology Office (USITO)
George Shea, Managing Director
Rm. 332 3/F Lido Office Tower, Lido Place, Jiang Tai Road, Beijing 100004, China
Tel: (86-10) 6430-1368-72
Fax: (86-10) 6430-1367
www.usito.org

U.S. Embassy Contacts

U.S. Embassy Beijing
No. 3 Xiu Shui Beijie, Beijing 100600, China
Tel: (86-10) 6532-3831
http://beijing.usembassy-china.org.cn

Mailing Address from U.S.:
U.S. Embassy Beijing
Department of State
Washington, DC 20521-7300
Ambassador's Office
Clark T. Randt, Jr.
Tel: (86-10) 6532-3831, x6400
Fax: (86-10) 6532-6422

Economic Section
Minister-Counselor for Economic Affairs: James Zumwalt
Tel: (86-10) 6532-3831 x6539
Fax: (86-10) 6532-6422

U.S. Commercial Service
Minister-Counselor for Commercial Affairs: Lee Boam
Tel: (86-10) 8529-6655 x801
Fax: (86-10) 8529-6558
Deputy: Denny Barnes
Tel: (86-10) 8529-6655 x802
Fax: (86-10) 8529-6558

| # Information and Contacts

Foreign Agricultural Service
Agricultural Affairs Office
Minister-Counselor for Agricultural Affairs: Larry Senger
Tel: (86-10) 6532-1953
Fax: (86-10) 6532-2962

Shanghai Agricultural Trade Office
Attache: Laverne E. Brabant
Tel: (86-21) 6279-8622
Fax: (86-21) 6279-8336

Guangzhou Agricultural Trade Office
Dr. Sam Wong
Tel: (86-20) 8667-7553
Fax: (86-20) 8666-0703

Animal and Plant Health Inspection Service
Attache: Dale Maki
Tel: (86-10) 6505-4575
Fax: (86-10) 6505-4574

American Consulate General Chendu
No. 4 Lingshiguan Road, Section 4, Renmin Nanlu, Chengdu 610041, China
Consul General: David Bleyle
Tel: (86-28) 8555-3119
Fax: (86-28) 8558-3520

Commercial Officer
Tel: (86-28) 8558-3992
Fax: (86-28) 8558-9221

American Consulate General Guangzhou

No. 1 South Shamian Street, Guangzhou 510133, China
Consul General: John J. Norris
Tel: (86-20) 8121-8000
Fax: (86-20) 8121-6296
Principal Commercial Officer: Ned Quistorff
Tel: (86-20) 8667-4011
Fax: (86-20) 8666-6409

American Consulate General Shanghai

1469 Huaihai Zhong Lu, Shanghai 200031, China
Consul General: Henry Levine
Tel: (86-21) 6433-6880
Fax: (86-21) 6433-4122
Principal Commercial Officer: Catherine Houghton
Tel: (86-21) 6279-7630
Fax: (86-21) 6279-7639

American Consulate General Shenyang

No. 52, 14th Wei Road
Heping District
Shenyang 110003, China
Consul General: Angus Simmons
Tel: (86-24) 2322-1198
Fax: (86-24) 2322 2374
Principal Commercial Officer: Erin Sullivan
Tel: (86-24) 2322-1198
Fax: (86-24) 2322-2206

U.S. Department of Commerce
International Trade Administration
Office of China Economic Area
Room 1229
1401 Constitution Avenue NW
Washington, DC 20230
Tel: (202) 482-3583
Fax: (202) 482-1576

Multilateral Development Bank Office
Brenda Ebeling, Director
Tel: (202) 482-3399
Fax: (202) 482-5179

U.S. Trade Promotion Coordinating Committee
Trade Information Center
Tel: 800-USA-TRADE

U.S. Department of State
Office of China and Mongolia
Bureau of East Asia and Pacific Affairs
Room 4318, 2201 C Street NW
Washington, DC 20520
Tel: (202) 647-6796
Fax: (202) 647-6820

Office of Business Affairs
Tel: (202) 746-1625
Fax: (202) 647-3953

Appendix 16 | Information and Contacts

U.S. Department of Agriculture
International Trade Policy
Asia American Division
Foreign Agricultural Service
Stop 1023
1400 Independence Avenue SW
Washington, DC 20250-1023
Tel: (202) 720-1289
Fax: (202) 690-1093
E-mail: *deatonl@fas.usda.gov*

AgExport Services Division
Foreign Agricultural Service
Ag Box 1052
1400 Independence Avenue SW
Washington, DC 20250-1052
Tel: (202) 720-6343
Fax: (202) 690-4374

Trade Assistance and Promotion Office
Tel: (202) 720-7420

Office of U.S. Trade Representative
China Desk
600 17th Street NW
Washington, DC 20506
Tel: (202) 395-5050
Fax: (202) 395-3911

Export-Import Bank of the United States
Business Development Office
Washington, DC 20571
Tel: 202-565-3900
Fax: 202-565- 3946
www.exim.gov

Beijing Contact: Douglas Lee
E-mail: *Douglas.Lee@mail.doc.gov*

Index